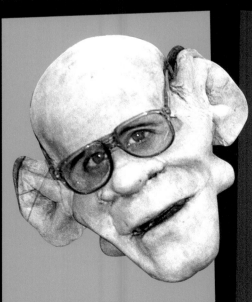
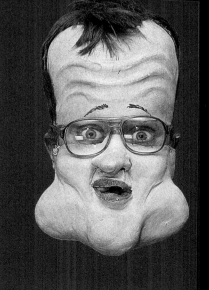

Transworld Publishers / 61–63 Uxbridge Road, London W5 5SA / a division of The Random House Group Ltd
Random House Australia (PTY) Ltd / 20 Alfred Street, Milsons Point, Sydney, New South Wales 2061, Australia
Random House New Zealand Ltd / 18 Poland Road, Glenfield, Auckland 10, New Zealand
Random House South Africa (PTY) Ltd / Endulini, 5a Jubilee Road, Parktown 2193, South Africa

Published 2004 by Channel 4 Books, a division of Transworld Publishers / Copyright © Leigh Francis 2004

Design by M2 www.mtwo.co.uk. Printed in Germany / 1 3 5 7 9 10 8 6 4 2

Papers used by Transworld Publishers are natural, recyclable products made from wood grown in sustainable forests. The manufacturing processes conform to the environmental regulations of the country of origin.

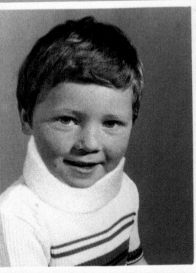

Book Selecta!

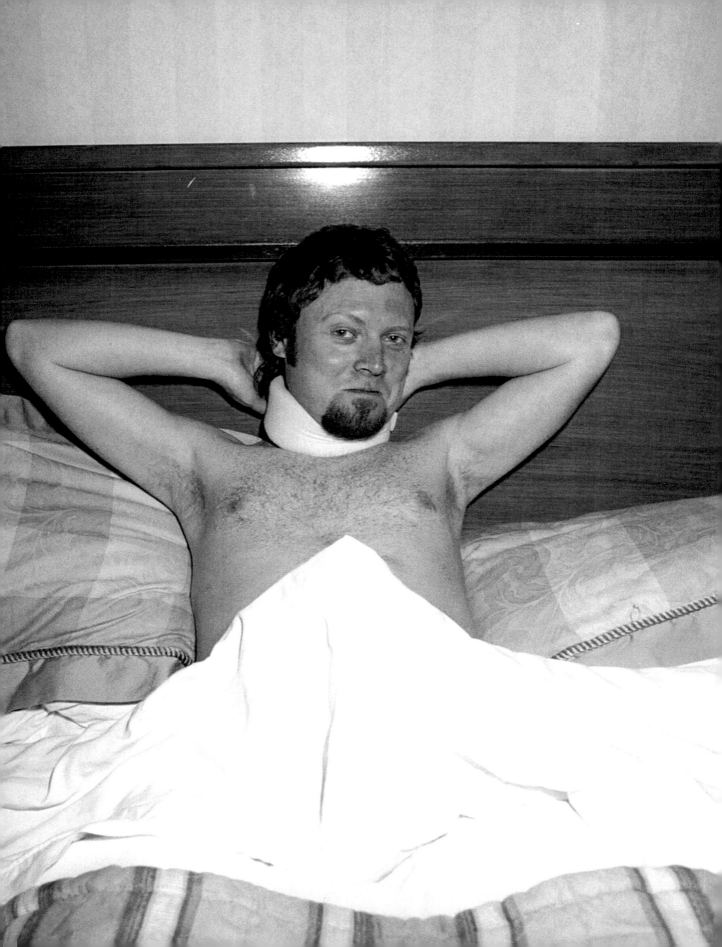

Some of the times and dates in this biographical look at most of my imaginary life are wrong. Names have been changed to protect the innocent. Some of what I've written is bullshit, and some of the gays and lesbians who I've mentioned are not really gays or lesbians, so stop crying about it. Just like Ulrika Jonsson, I won't mention who did it to me. And what else?...er... ah yes! Don't worry Sean Pertwee, son of the genius Jon Pertwee who scared the crap out of me with his portrayal of a living SCARECROW, I won't mention the story you told me about Stella McCartney stealing your father's prop robin red breast that he used to keep in his belly when he was WORZEL GUMMIDGE. oops...

HELLO TO YOU!

To start, I would like to say thank you please to the U.K. garage sensation Craig David and indeed Artful Dodger. Without these people I never would have heard of the word BO! SELECTA!! which, for anybody who doesn't know, means "good DJ", and has no relevance to a man wearing a rubber mask. Well it does now, but it didn't back in 1999. So thank you please, and I apologise to Craig David for any grief you have experienced due to me wearing a rubber mask of you and giving you the persona of a bed-wetting kestrel lover. HEY! While I'm at it, I apologise to Michael Jackson for portraying you as a bad-mouthed, pimp gangster; Mel B as a working class bean-flicker; Gareth Gates for the hep, hep, heps; Lorraine Kelly for giving you a massive GROWLER and Mick Hucknall for the long lady-touching arm. But by far the worst of my torments is Kat Slater with her big flabby bingo wings. Everyone I do on BO' SELECTA! I have nothing but respect for and have imagined you have all drank my sex wee as part of love-making at one point in my sick, demented little life.

I LOVE YOU ALL IN THE FACE. TWICE.

So to you the reader, thank you please to you also, for buying my book and watching BO' SELECTA! It's been an incredible ride that I hope you have enjoyed as much as I have, and the team that make the show (thank you please to you lot of dirty, pervy bastards). I'm brown-nosing now, but thank you please to Channel 4 for giving ~~me~~ a twisted Arachnipusian obsessive the chance to live his wet dreams out for real and meet so many lovely celebrities; Davina McCall, The Osbournes, Jonathan Ross, Patsy Kensit, Mel B, Craig David, Emma Bunton, Ronan Keating, Denise Van Outen, Liberty X and many, many more beautiful celebrities...

I always dreamed that **_Kylie Minogue_** was my wife, she would make my dinner, do my ironing and then at the end of the day I would r**ide her like Seabiscuit**. But I never could have dreamed that you would be sat here reading my book. I hope it don't going to be shit for you. If it is shit, don't read it, just look at the pictures. There's more pictures than writing anyway, so if you are thick as shit, don't worry, you don't need brains to read this. If you're like me it's just going to be an endless bank of toss that you can use at your leisure. Actually, I wanted to have one of the centre pages laminated so you can do a sex wee on it and wipe it off, but they said it was too bloody fucking expensive. Of course, if you are a lady you just flick your bean. But don't you worry, there is both a wank page for a man and a lady. I won't tell you who the wank pictures are of yet, because at this moment I don't know. I've never written a book before, I'm making it up as I go along. Just like the TV show and my whole television career to date.

So here it is, **<u>BOOK'SELECTA!</u>**, deep inside, from behind. It's basically going to be the story of what has happened to me. Like Geri Halliwell's biography when she tell you how she used to be a bit trampy living in a squat hole until she became so rich as a Spice Girl that she could shit pound coins. I can't shit pound coins, but things have definitely changed. Like just the other night, I had dinner with *Patsy Kensit* and *Lisa Stansfield*. I sat there all night munching on meat with a dick so hard I could cut butter with it! (The Bear said that once to Jamie Oliver). I don't think I'm mental, I'm just very passionate about the things I like. Male or female, celabrites are my muse, my outlet, my addiction, my object of desire; they are my life.

So let me tell you how it all started. I sound mental as a shit with eyes that can talk don't I? Take everything I say with a pinch of salt.

A long time ago, in a galaxy far, far away...

I was born in Arachnipus, just outside Transylvania, when I was no years of age. Not many people have heard of Arachnipus, that's why I often just say I'm from Transylvania, home to the Cheeky Girls. A threesome would be great with those two Cheekies, if they both ate a bit of dinner. I worry for them sometimes, they're both very thin, then I stop worrying and have a moment with myself. By the way, I apologise for all my wank talk, but it's natural, we all do it, it's science. Even girls do it, but they don't admit it, but I like that about ladies. If they admitted they did it, they would be the same as us boys with hard tissues under our beds. Or they would be **<u>Abi Titmuss</u>**. I saw it on the internet.

Anyway, in Arachnipus my mother made a lot of money from being a sexy lady for men to enjoy, and that's all I will say about that. As for my father, I never met him, but my mother would tell me he was a Dracula impersonator. He would be booked for hen nights and would wear a cape and nothing else. He was like one of those Chippendale men things, but really rubbish.

As a child, I would dress as Dracula myself. In Arachnipus Dracula is bigger than Will Young, he is the man! I remember I would walk around dressed as Dracula, just like my father (although I never met him). I think my first obsession was Spider-Man. I still like him very much now. Does that sound gay? Fuck it! I think gays are great! It's a shame for them, most of them dress really well and are very handsome and could get any woman they want. But they prefer to just go shopping with them and have their potackayans rubbed by men. Anyway, back to Spider-Man. He's not really a celabrity, but at that age I didn't really know many celabrities, apart from **David Bowie**, who I had a poster of on my wall. It was a picture of him with orange hair. I think my mother bought it for me to make me feel normal. As we all know, there are not many redheads in Arachnipus. Maybe you don't know. Well, I'm telling you: there isn't.

Yes, I remember I would go to school in my Spider-Man suit under my real clothes and sweat more than Rick Waller on a treadmill. I suppose my neck brace didn't help. Fuck! I just thought, that's probably how the teachers knew it was me. My neck brace! How could I have been so stupid? Oh yes, by the way – that whole story of how I got my neck injury when Lisa Tarbuck punched me in the neck and called me a son of a bitch because I told her she look better in trousers than a skirt; it's a slight elaboration. It's true that I met her at a Hollyoaks party and I told her she was brilliant! But she didn't punch me, she just told me to stop brown nosing her. Anyone who knows me knows that's the truth. She probably don't remember though.

The neck brace; well, I've always worn one. I suppose it's like a comfort blanket. I feel naked without it. It's also a good conversation piece. You can make elaborate stories up about how you got it. Just like the one I just told you. Or like the time I said I was kicked off of **SARA COX**'s Channel 4 show 'Born Sloppy'. I tried to handcuff myself to her and she flipped out and did a karate chop on me. That really happened! She didn't karate chop me, but I did get kicked off the show for trying to handcuff myself to her. What better way to show my love to her? I still love her. **I love Cox!**

As I got older, I remember having a big obsession for **_Michael Jackson_**. I would watch the Thriller video on a loop, shitting myself. I had Michael Jackson dolls and my mother made me a jacket just like the one Michael Jackson wore in Thriller, I'd later pick one up from a second-hand shop in Camden Town, London, England for 60 English pounds. Who would have thought that I would end up wearing it on television? **Derren Brown** probably knew because he is a wizard who can see into the future, that fucking genius.

I enjoyed my childhood in Arachnipus. My mother's ten and a half brothers were in construction and, because she was quite an eccentric, she had them build our home on top of a wooden hill. It sounds fucking mental, doesn't it? Well, it was. I don't know why she had it done, I suppose it was to show how well she had done, a sign of her achievement. Wow, this is quite serious, isn't it? I'm going to skip some shit and get straight to the stuff you'll probably be more interested in.

SO HOW DID A GINGER TIT LIKE ME GET ON TV?

I had been living in England for about eight English years. I didn't work because work would interfere with my hobby – stalking. Although I didn't consider myself a stalker, stalkers are crazy people that wank too much because they live by themselves. I still don't consider myself a stalker.

I didn't need to work because I inherited a small fortune from my mother, I can't tell you how she got so financially big-cocked, but it has something to do with the reason I had to leave Arachnipus. It's a sensitive subject just like John Leslie and Abi Titmuss.

Anyhow, because I didn't work I spent a lot of time watching television and grew a fondness for _**Richard and Judy**_. It's not that I'm a massive fan of theirs, or most celabrities for that matter, I don't know what it is, it's just a thrill to meet people that are famous. Don't get me wrong, I love them and would enjoy it if they sat on my face so I could see their details, it's just that I couldn't tell you everything about them, although I could tell you more than most people, but not as much as their mothers or fathers. What the fuck am I going on about? Right, I was obsessed by Richard and Judy and I am a massive fan – I would stick cardboard cut-outs of their faces to mannequins and imagine I was on 'This Morning' like a mental tit with two nipplets. I started to follow them. I would hang outside the London Weekend Television, outside The Ivy, buy tickets for premieres that I knew they were attending. But I never had the confidence to speak to them. I could only speak to my mannequins. Because my English wasn't so good back then, it made me shy like the Elephant Man, that poor bastard was made out of pork pies, terrible.

I started going to book signings, it was amazing! I couldn't believe it, for the price of a book you could get to meet the celebrity you've always dreamed of putting your wet upon. I never came across Richard and Judy doing a book signing, but they were small fish compared to Louise Nurding/the whitey from Eternal/Redknapp. She was doing a signing at HMV for one of her albums. This was the first signing I ever recorded with my video camera. Louise is more sexy than eight hot dogs in brine.

Louise makes me feel like a Jack Russell in season.

Legs all brown I'd like to kiss

My pants are wet, I've done a sex piss,

Her teeth so white, whiter than snow,

They fucking are, they are you know,

I write a poem but I am shit,

I kiss her cheek, I kiss her tit.

Tit, titty, titty, tit!

Thank you please, Louise.

So I was in the queue for about one hour. A lady from 'Liquid News' (that used to be on BBC 3 before it was axed for some reason – I loved that show with *Claudia Winkleman* and her interesting eyes) interviewed me and asked me what it was that I liked about Louise. As straightforward as I always am, I told her "I really like her song 'Naked', and I always think of her naked. I wish she would rape me." Sometimes I say things I shouldn't. What I meant was, I think she is a great talent and very pretty to boot! So anyway, as I got closer to Louise I became so nervous that maybe she wouldn't like my gift of a carriage clock that I got from Argos, that a bit of shit came out of my ass. No it didn't, it did. As I got closer the security spotted me and shit themselves (there's a lot of shit happening here, right?). "What have you got in your package?" they asked. "I'm not mental," I said, "what the fuck do you think it is? It's carriage clock-shaped." She looked quite pleased with my gift, I got a kiss from her and I told her I would love to make love to her. It was a lot more exciting if you were there.

I went home and stuck a cut-out of **LOUISE** to a mannequin and washed its tits.

Jamie Oliver

Jamie Oliver is very cool,

He is cooler than the water in a swimming pool,

His hair is pukka, his lisp is cute,

I'd like to see him in his birthday suit,

and share the crap house with him, I bet even his shit smells as good as his cooking.

Jamie Oliver

I met Jamie at Virgin Records when he was signing his book, I gave him a carriage
gave him a second clock at Clinton Cards that same day as he was signing his cal
weeks later I caught up with him at Waterstone's book store and give him a tin of s
beans and invited him to my flat. He didn't come, the bastard. So I had a sick fanta
and I cut off his ear just like that naughty bad man did to that copper in 'Reservoir

Barbara Windsor was nice. She was signing her book at Harrods where I repeate
for a kiss and gave her a shit portrait of a woman that I picked up from a charity sh
was of my dead mother who was an even bigger fan of Babs than me when she w
she is dead, but when she was alive she thought Babs was on the perfect! But no
and she was back then when I met Barbara Windsor. My mother has been dead f
her, though. I like her, she is nice.

So I kept on going to these book signings, 80s lispy pop star *Toyah Willcox*, **Pa**
MARTINE MCCUTCHEON… whenever there was a signing I was there. I wasn'
was, it just felt like such an achievement for me to meet these people that were
in their presence. All of these meetings were recorded on my camcorder and air
show a called 'Show Me The Funny' on E4, in which viewers got to vote for the s
to see in its entirety, from a selection of other sketches made by other comedian
that were played on the internet.

I've never felt I was a comedian, I don't do a stand up thing where you say, "take my wife", cos I don't have one, and I didn't really see my short films or 'sketches' as sketches. To me, they were serious documentations of my celabrity confrontations, not supposed to be funny. But people were voting to see them, and if people thought they were funny, fuck it, so be it. The more people voted to see them, the more I got the chance to make them and meet more celabs, and I quite liked the fact people were watching and enjoying my tapes because, like I said, to me, meeting a celab is a great achievement.

Things were changing. I now had a job making things for television. It wasn't porno, but it was very close to it. Meeting all these celabs was better than doing a sex for me. It was an incredible rush, like snow boarding when you bash your balls up so they go blue.

Channel 4 liked the stuff I did on E4 so much, they asked if I'd like to do my own show. If it meant I got to meet celabrities, then YES, I would love to do it. Although I never thought I would become a celabrity myself, what the fuck was I going to do, sit at home and chase my own tail like a little dog and lick my balls?

THIS IS THE STANGEST PICTURE, "MYSELF AS A DOG LICKING MY OWN BALL'S" DRAWN IN BIRO (A PEN OBTAINED FROM WALT DISNEY RESORTS)

THE PILOT

So, a pilot was commissioned. If it went well, Channel 4 would commission a series. I never thought this would happen to me. I was shitting in my pants, although I don't know why, because I didn't plan any of this so if it went all wrong, shit fuck it. I'll go back to doing my home videos, because that's what I did anyway. I was a professional obsessive, a super-fan. Who was I kidding? Yes! I was a fucking stalker and I still am to this very day. I say some rude shit sometimes, but I don't mean no harm. I just like celabs. Is that a crime?

I am normal.

AVID MERRION'S 10 steps to a healthy life

←X2

1. Always wear two pairs of pants. This is good to make your prick bulge bigger and it is also handy if you shit your pants.

2. Don't ever start watching a film after twelve o'clock; it's too late. You could fall asleep and miss the titty bit. Only stay up if it's a really good film like 'Teen Wolf'. Forget 'Teen Wolf 2' though, starring Jason Bateman; it's crap and there's no titties in it.

3. When eating out at a fancy restaurant, if you are full like a fatty and feel you have to leave a little bit, mess up your left-over food, otherwise these restaurant bastards will probably serve your left-overs to some other poor bitch. You know, like your left-over salad garnish.

4. Never trust a man with two hairstyles. Even though at the moment I kind of have two hairstyles myself (short on top, long at the back like one of those fucking mullet things – I haven't had time to get it cut). Anyway, never trust a man who has two hairstyles. If he can't decide on a simple thing such as a hairstyle, how can he be relied on to decide on anything else, the useless pig! I knew a man once that couldn't decide whether to have a side-parting or a middle-parting. His life was a mess.

5. Toss off at least once a day. Apparently it can help prevent prostate cancer – what better reason do you need to vigorously make love to yourself?

6. Even though Gail Porter don't get her crack out any more, don't forget about her. Always remember that FHM cover and she will stay in that toss bank for many years to come.

7. If somebody hates you, like them even more. Hopefully, they will be so confused that you still like them, even though they treat you like shit, that they will kill themselves, the silly naughty bastards.

8. Don't say anything bad about Michael Jackson until we have hard evidence! Even though his face has gone a bit funny, he is still the king of pop.

9. Soapy wanks are not good for you. When in the shower, never be tempted to do a soapy toss. As the jap's eye opens to shoot your sexy thick piss, soap will go down it and sting like a twat. It might feel good at the beginning when it's all soaped up, but the end result is not worth the stinging pain.

10. Try not to be nasty to people, it's just wasted energy. Just go home and draw a really good detailed picture of them being murdered by a giant clown with fangs and a tommy gun.

For the pilot I was going to show my appreciation for celabrites using rubber masks. I can't do impressions, but I can do different voices. I've always said it was someone else doing the masks because I'm too shy to do the voices without the masks. So they built a set of my flat. It was incredible. It was just like it, but I don't have toss tissues under my bed. I put them in a sock. Well, I used to. I wanted to make a female Guy Fawkes filled with my sex wee tissues with the face of **_Kylie Minogue_**. Then, on second thoughts, it was too pervert. I'm not a pervert, I don't think. Anyway, apart from toss tissues, it was just like my flat.

So I would come in and talk about celabrities, show my camcorder tapes and do links for the mask stuff. I was shit because I don't do this before. There were cameras everywhere, and I don't know which one to look at. I was like Rain Man; "Five cameras, five cameras, definitely five cameras."

Craig David would come on to the set – not the real one, the mask one – and say, "When I say Bo, say Selecta!". Michael Jackson would challenge a viewer to eat as many Weetabix as he could, and the real Davina McCall would be the guest. It was really strange, but so much fun that I had to keep going to the toilet to empty myself. **_Davina McCall_** was **beeeautiful like a plate full of sausage**. She told a story about a contestant that she had on a show she used to do called 'God's Gift'. The contestant for some reason was just wearing a thong, but he had a little bit of shit in it. Lucky for Davina, I had that exact thong on to remind her of that shitty experience. I pulled my pants down to reveal my shit covered crack. It wasn't really shit, it was Nutella. But it was a great feeling shoving my Nutella covered arse in her face. I love Davina McCall, she has a big sexy French nose. I would love to suck it. There was no sign of the Bear in the pilot, I'd not met him yet. That happened much later, I think he was busy doing some show on satellite television.

The pilot was shot before an audience that were all dressed as their favourite celabrities. Matthew Wright from Channel Five's 'The Wright Stuff' judged the best costume. He came on inside a large mirror on wheels. He was the 'Mirror Of Truth'. The truth was he was pissed as a fart, just like **JESSIE WALLACE** when you see her in the tabloids. Don't you think she has sexy eyes? I do, not like Matthew Wright. He had a face like Popeye all pissed up. But he is a great sport and a very funny man.

The masks for the show were, and still are, made by Steve Webster. He'd made a lot of props for Vic & Bob's 'Shooting Stars'. I love Vic Reeves and Bob Mortimer, they make me laugh so much I wet like a lady. Isn't it weird that ladies actually piss sometimes when they can't control their laughter?

So I would design the bulk of the masks and send drawings to Steve. He would bring them into the office and I was amazed! They were just like the drawings. The masks were made out of rubber latex and lined with foam. Some are more comfortable than others, it depend on how long you are wearing it for. Sometimes it would feel like you have your head inside a sweaty asshole. So obviously I had my favourites – Craig David and Michael Jackson were my favourites at that time. The first time I did Craig David it was for a segment called Craig David's Day Off, I also did Michael Jackson's Day Off, Eminem's Day Off, Sting's Day Off and Geri's Day Off. Craig David wasn't the UK garage sensation we know today, and not many people were familiar with the sound of his voice when he talk, which was good, because I can't do a Southampton accent. Is there one? Anyway, I gave him a voice that I thought fit with the mask and it seemed to work. **Proper Bo!, I tell thee.**

CRAIG

REETO, CRAAAAAIG DAAAAVID HERE IN A BOOK'SELECTA!

And it's proper Bo!, I tell thee. As you can see, there's a variety of pictures of meself, all colourful like!

I've had our Kes for about four year now. When I got her she was only a egg, which, for anybody who doesn't know, is the proper name for a baby kestrel. I got her from a man in Huddersfield who had a dog with one leg called Uni. She only cost me a pound, so she was a right bargain. Mind you, I don't think you should put a price on summat like a bird of prey. They're priceless, aren't they? Well, they're not cos like I said, our Kes cost me a pound, but yer know what I mean, don't yer? It's a privilege that she actually allows me to own her. Sitting there all still for't cameras. She's as Bo! as they come, in't she? I reet love her, I do, I tell thee. Bastard, I've pissed meself. I'll go put me piss sack on and I shall appear in this book later. Bo' Selecta!

SERIES ONE

So, after a long wait, Channel 4 finally decided they would like to commission the show. The format changed a little; instead of filming it before an audience in a studio, we decided to film it in my actual flat, just like 'The Osbournes'! **I fucking love <u>the Osbournes</u>**, especially *Kelly*. I think she is so cool, she is the same colour as white bread, a little bit tubby on the telly, but in real life she is less tubby. I met her once. She told me to go fuck you to me. One of the best days of my life. Thank you please Kelly Osbourne.

Channel 4 were a little concerned that nobody would know who I was, so before we started filming for the show, they asked if I would do some little bits for Big Brother 3 to play out on E4. That way it would introduce a television audience to me. So I said yes! I was loving Big Brother and was a big fan of *Jade Goody*, so I spent two days in a tiny flat that was supposed to be like mine, talking to mannequins with the housemates heads stuck on. Nothing out of the ordinary there, so I don't get nervous. We approached the Craig from Big Brother 1 to do some stuff. I'd met him a few times before. When I say "met", I mean "stalked". I hounded him at a signing at Sock Shop in London. He was signing his single at that time of year called 'At This Time Of Year'. Maybe the fact that he was signing in a shop that sold socks rather than CDs was probably the reason his song didn't do too well. He was shit scared of me at first, but once he realised that I was no danger we became good friends and he became my friend in the cupboard! I got to go down to the Big Brother studios, it was amazing! I had to tape my prick down so nobody know how excited I was. I was there on the eviction night. I met Jade's mother, she was great fun. She was the nicest one-armed lesbian I ever met. I never met a one-armed lesbian before. But after I meet Jade's mother, I have to say; one armed lesbians are one of the nicest people you can meet. Unless you can meet Dermot O'Leary or **Davina McCall**. It was so strange that they knew who I was. These are people that in my mind I have, well you know – we have exchanged fluids. Davina is one of my favourite ladies on telly, I wrote her a poem:

Davina

Lovely Davina,

Have you seen her?

In the cantina,

Drinking Ribena,

I could never be keener,

To show her my wiener,

It's never been cleaner,

Oh lovely Davina,

More sexy than Xena

The warrior princess that used to be on Channel 5 who looked like she could be a lesbian. If she only had one arm she'd probably be one of the nicest one armed lesbians you could meet!

That's a shit poem, right? I don't care, sometimes it is good for me to express myself with a poem. It stops me from doing a toss.

Oh lovely Davina.

While down at the **BB** studios it was so strange that even the crowds knew who I was. This is a man that has spent most of his life making love to himself at home or outside in the rain waiting for just a glimpse of a celab and there I was doing a chat with _**Graham Norton**_ who also was campaigning for Jade, even though he didn't want to put his wet on her like I did. It's a common fact that he is a fudge packer and that's why we love him. He's a big funny fudge packer like Elton John!

Men I'd

Elton John's

BEAU
SELECTION

like to *Bum*

1. Matt Goss...

...from Bros and Hell's Kitchen. I loved him when he used to be in Bros. He was always well turned-out, just like one of us. Oh, when he sang 'Drop the boy', that's right boy, drop them! Drop them! Let's have a look at your dangles. I'll bum you into next week!

2. Brian McFadden...

...for his lovely big hands, especially as he doesn't need them for his wife's massive boobs any more! Kerry McFadden's children will never go hungry, not with those big tits. Brian, you have my number – call me.

3. Duncan ...

...from Blue. The ladies love him, the gays love him, I bet even puppy dogs love him. He can smoke on my old fella anytime he chooses.

4. Kevin Webster ...

...from Coronation Street. Leave Sally, Kevin, come stay with me. But grow your 'tache back. I love the feeling of a man's 'tache on my bum.

5. Peter Andre ...

...Bring Jordan, she can watch, maybe I could teach her how to really please a man.

6. Justin Timberlake ...

...Even though he looks like Screech from 'Saved By The Bell', there's just something about him. Of course, he's got the moves and he can sing, but maybe with a little hand I could help him reach those high notes. Or maybe with a big hand. It depends on how accommodating he is. Lovely little arse crack.

7. John Leslie ...

...Tall and handsome; an all round catch.
A nice man you could bring home to your mother.
But don't leave him alone with her. The man just can't resist!

8. Any man ...

...from Hollyoaks!

9. Will Young ...

...A nice talented young man, fresh and ready to eat.

10. Nadia ...

...from BB5. Sometimes it's good to experiment!

So with my dead mother all wrapped up in clingfilm in my wardrobe (an old Arachnipusian saying goes: "If you love them, don't stick them in the ground with the shit and worms. Keep them in the wardrobe close to where you sleep, but use Magic Trees so they don't stink of shit." Isn't that a strange saying?) and with Craig chained up in the cupboard (he always had the key, he just wanted to be on television) we began filming the first episode.

Even though Big Brother had introduced me to a television audience, not too many people knew who I was, so I could still go about my business, sneaking in the shadows and mixing with other celab fans like myself. Celab fans give strange presents, but none more stranger than me. I don't know how many times I have given someone a flask of my sex wee. I mean, how much love does that show? You love yourself all week thinking about, I don't know, Davina McCall, and you give them that love in a flask. That show a lot of love for them, I think. Watch the smile on their beautiful face grow! It's the best present you can give, it's the truth. That or a hot water bottle, or should I say a hot sex wee bottle? So yes, the Davina McCall was the first guest. **Thank you please, Davina**. There I sat, wearing a large nose made out of masking tape pretending to be her. I told her straight I would love to see her take a shit. Since that day people have shouted that at me in the street. But it's OK, I like them. We also had the lovely Jade on the show straight from the BB house. I bumped into her while buying baps and milk. I give her my baps as a gift and, you know what?, I think I made her day. When a man approaches you in the street and gives you baps, that's something special, right? *Liberty X* featured in the show as well, with the naughty little Bear.

hELLO RASI-CLARTS welcome to my

bit in this shit book. This book should've been mine and all about me! Why? Cos I'm the best thing that ever happened to this show. I don't know how that ginger bollocks gets a book deal, and speaking of ginger bollocks, because of my contract I have an obligation to mention that knob jockey Steven.

Squeak, squeak, squeak, squeak, squeak, squeak squeak, squeak squeak, squeaksqueak, squeaksqueak, squeaksqueak, squeaksqueak, squeaksqueak, squeak!

Oh! Do you know what Steven just wrote? He wrote that this book is getting boring, so why don't they just have some pictures of some good boobies? And I agree! So let's have some. Yeah! Brilliant! The next page has boobs on it. This book might be worth reading after all.

That was nice, wasn't it? A nice page of boobies. Wouldn't this book have been better with a read-along tape for some of the people who can't read? You know, like the thick kids that do special English at school. Then there could have been soundbites and extracts from the show - just the bits that I'm in, of course. Anyway, let me tell you about me and my success. As an orphan I play on it just to get sympathy from pretty girls. Most bears are orphans anyway, but luckily for me most bears can't talk. Yes, there's been talking bears on the telly before, but none of them were real. They didn't have cocks, and if it can't piss it ain't real. That's a fact so shut up.

How I joined the show was an accident. The pilot had a different director.

Avid - Tom Pool, a very nice man.

Bear - Piss off Avid, you brown-nosing fuck face. This is my bit, and seeing as it's my bit, can the graphic design be a bit better? I want my bits to look untold, yeah?

So, the director that took over from that other one was this gay that I was working with on a project called Bear Fax. He says he isn't gay, but do bears shit in the woods? Yes they do, but I don't cos I'm very advanced. So advanced I can set a video recorder. "Wow, so what?" I hear you say. But what fucking animal do you know that can set a video, eh? Right, eat my arse out, you knob jockey.

Anyway, my project didn't come off for some reason, and I was given a slot in Bo' Selecta! Should've been called Bear' Selecta!, really. I was happy to come in and make the show a bit more funniererer. Liberty X were my first guests. Nice people. They had a sexy video that I'd tampered with. You know, just cut all the rubbish bits out and kept all the good bits in. Boob shots and bums. Hey, I was trying to help them. Sex sells, doesn't it? So there I was,

and I just couldn't control myself, out popped my tail. I was ever so embarrassed. It had never happened before. But the makers of the programme seemed to like it. So I made sure it popped out every week. Even if it was someone that I didn't really fancy, like Christine Hamilton. Honestly, She was like my mum. But with less hair and a smaller nose, roughly the same age though, and liked her little tipple. I think she had a bottle of wine before she came up the tree house. Tried to grab my tail she did, dirty old tail grabber!

Who else? Tess Daly, or Tess Kay as she's known now she's married to Vernon Kay. That's right, she has the name of a supermarket. Tesskay! Beat our prices! And we'll beat you, you bastards! Ha! Ha! Ha! Tess was sexy, a lot shyer than I imagined, and I mean I was pretty young back then, so it's not as if I was going to come out with some crude remark that she wouldn't understand. Like I would now. I know I'm rude and I swear too much, but it's my upbringing. I'm actually trying to stop swearing so I can appeal to a wider audience. Don't worry, I'm not changing my style, just a little less fucks. Yeh, it was weird in the beginning how many of my guests seemed a little nervous. I think they were just amazed. Most people haven't come across a talking bear before; Sarah Cawood, Terri Dwyer, Kate Thornton… they were all amazed and, to be honest with you, I am, I'm pretty amazing!

Of course, in the second and third series people were a bit more used to me. I don't really know how I acquired the power of speech, but hey, nobody questioned Howard The Duck, did they? Bloody 'ell, maybe I'm an alien bear that was adopted by a regular bear family and when they learned of my gift of speech they shit themselves that I was going to reveal to the human race their plan for taking over the world, just like in 'Planet Of The Apes'. Good story teller ain't I? That's why in the second series I suggested that's what I do; tell bedtime stories. My most memorable would have to be the time Jonathan Ross came over. I remember the story well. It was very brief, I just wanted him to say words beginning with 'R' for obvious reasons. Don't get me wrong, I think he's a genius. I see a lot of myself in

The Bear

This is him
stood up.

loose arms
with wire in
them

wire in
hands so
we can bend
finger

moveable
legs so
we can
sit him
down.

This him
sat down.

MR. Big's
own line
of crap
trainers

him, you know, but I'm younger. I'm sure he can see that I'm a bit like him, and he's given me a lot of tips. Nothing I didn't know already. But yeh, Rossy is one of the main ones, like me. Me and Ross are the main ones. So anyway, back to the story…

"Once upon a time there was a cuddly little bear that lived in a tree house on Hampstead Heath. One day, something really strange happened. The bear looked out of his window and saw something rude. Richard the rabbit was rampantly rogering the radiant rabbit Rachael in a field of rape seed oil whilst Ramone the robin red breast rubbed himself rapidly."

OK, so it wasn't an award-winning novel, but I only had a three-minute slot. The piece actually went on for about half an hour and was great fun. If I had a longer time slot, the story would have been longer. A best-selling book, no doubt. It would have had Panda Anderson in it and I would have saved her from a big nasty man. I would have had a shooter and been all dope and rad! And when I saved her, a little bit of her nipple would have popped out as we escaped down a big mountain from the bad man's hide out who was pushing drugs on to kids that made them go stupid and mental so they would buy shit trainers that he'd designed. They were his own line of sportswear, you know, like when rappers bring out their own line of shit trainers. Stick to what you do best, yeh? So me and Panda escape cos that bad man had bear-napped her cos he wanted her to model his shit trainers, but she knew it wouldn't be best for her career. Anyway yeh, we escape with the help of Cameron Diaz (I can't think of a bear name for her, but in this story she's not a bear. She's Cameron Diaz from a sequel to 'Something about Mary' called 'Something Else About Mary', she can do karate so don't mess, you rast-clarts!). She kicks that bad man's dick in, I say thanks and kiss her. She falls in love with me from just that one kiss, but I say to her, "Look, I'd love to have sex with you, but I'm in love with Panda, and I didn't come all this way with that little Chinese boy from 'Raiders Of The Lost Ark' to risk my life trying

to save her, just to go wreck our relationship by having a meaningless fling with you Cameron." That Chinese boy is with me helping me along the way – use your imagination. So I say to Cameron, "Give me your number anyway, just in case Panda finishes with me and I'll call you then, OK, cos you are untold, you are fit as!" Panda overhears me say this to Cameron and dumps me. But I said it loud on purpose so she would hear me and dump me cos I like Cameron Diaz more, she is fitter than any woman I know, and I know lots.

So we fly home on that big eagle that was in Harry Potter (hate that geek). She does a dance in the front room of my new tree house that is massive and has a plasma screen in every room, even the piss pot room, and what she's wearing is those little Spider-Man underpants that she wore in 'Charlie's Angels'. Brilliant. Then just before she shows me her boobies, we're interrupted by a bloody knock at the door. I gently release Cameron's breast from my cute little bear paw, and see who it is who's rudely knocking at my front door right in the middle of my love scene when I'm just about to do Cameron up Diaz! And who is it? It's only bloody Ben Stiller still trying to get off with her from when he met her in 'There's Something About Mary'. I tell him straight: "Fuck off, she's mine! I'll be in one of your films, but Cameron is mine, so piss off you Zoolander bitch, before I do or say something I'll regret and regret it." And cos of the nipple and the bad language, there is a parental guidance sticker put on the front of the story book and kids flock to it. Cos adults, let me tell you something, kids love nipples and swearing! The End.

That's it. I'm bored. I might write something later. But you'd better put plenty of pictures of me in this book. This show would be nothing without me. Kids, enjoy the rest of it, you knob jockeys!

I met many of my favourite celabs in the first series; **_Penny Smith_** in her dressing room at GMTV, in which she got confused about the difference between a fangitta and a fajita (easy mistake to make – they both have beans, one you eat the other you flick); **_Michael Ball_**, who sang 'Happy Birthday' to my dead mother down the phone; **Vanessa Feltz**, who came to my birthday party and I sang her a song – "Lady of the night, cover me in shite, let me get inside your sweet fangitta!"; **_Keith Duffy_** from Boyzone, Celabrity Big Brother and Coronation Street, who I kissed mouth open while dressed as Vera Duckworth; Jenni Falconer, who smelled more nice than butter, who I impressed at the Inside Soap awards; **Mariella Frostrup** who I did my first chat show set-up with and asked her how she do a masturbate.

Throughout the series I would fantasise a lot about things I would like to do with celabs. I did bondage with **ETHAN HAWK**, I played with **KERRY MCFADDEN**'s massive tats and married Kylie Minogue and she had my bambino. Some of my fantasies I would live out using mannequins with celabs faces stuck on. Sometimes I would draw my fantasies in a segment called Avid's Art.

AVID'S ART

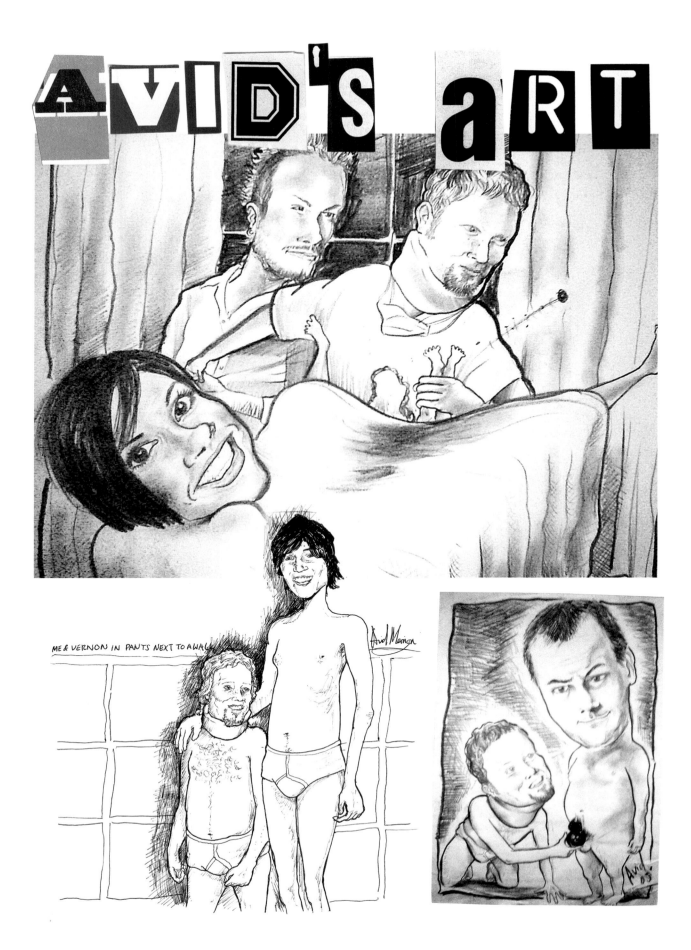

ME & VERNON IN PANTS NEXT TO A WALL

In episode four of series one, my neighbour and good friend Ozzy was introduced. Ozzy used to live downstairs from me and make me T-shirts. He is very kind and willing to make a prick of himself. Ozzy is not an actor, he has never been on television before, so I think he was pretty cool with the whole thing. Sometimes, when filming, it would take more than 16 times to get it right, but he is more foreign than me.

This was one of his lines: "I have brought you a T-shirt, it has Brad Pitt on it". That's what he was supposed to say, what he said was:

Take 1. "I have a shirt, it's got Brad pitta pa."

Take 2. "It's a shirt it's gotta pitta pa on it."

Take 3. "It's Brad pitta, what's a matter, you deaf? You're always like this."

Take 4. "What?"

Take 5. "Oh right! It's erm Brad pitta t-shirt"

I love Ozzy! He's on the perfect!

MICHAEL JACKASS

CHA'MONE MOTHAFUCKA!

I'm Michael Jackson, that's right. Y'all seen my childhood? I can't find that bastard cha'mone. So Bo' Selecta! introduced y'all to a side a of MJ that y'all ain't seen before. Like, I actually live next door to the Osbournes, those noisy bastards. Well, I used to, 'til I got my bad ass in a prison cell with Ronney Barkey' for being Bad, Off The Wall, Invincible and Dangerous. Dat's ma albums right there.

HEE, HEE, OW!

So check it out, let's talk about the good old days. When MJ used to do all that Jackass shit. **Cha'mone**, that was some ruthless shit right there, brother. Blind Boxing with Bubbles, y'all know I ain't talking about the monkey. I'm talking about ma fine pussy tang, tang. Bitch ain't got an inch of hair on her body. Goddamn that was a some fun right there. I hit the bitch in the face. She was real angry mothafucka. But y'all gotta understand sometimes people gonna get hurt doing this shit. Dat's why y'all shouldn't try dat shit at home mothafucka!

Cricket bat in the nuts, **cha'mone**. That hurt me real bad. The only pleasure I gotta out of dat shit was the fact we didn't have a full set of cricketey whites for Bubbles. She just do it in her T-shirt, but if y'all got it mothafucka, flaunt it mothafucka! Hee, hee!. Kiss ma bad self.

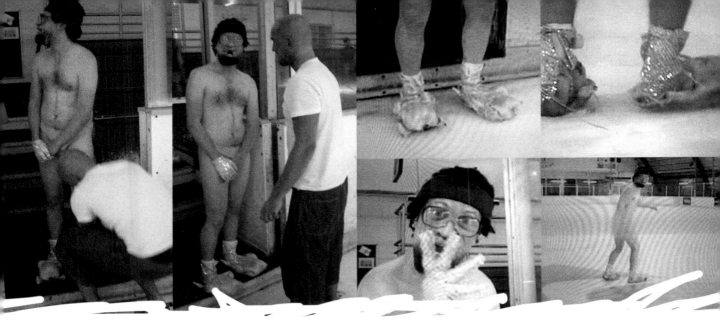

The most effectey gotta be the Naked Chicken Skatey! A lot of mothafuckas dig that shit. But falling on my black or white ass on dat ice, cha'mone, it hurt real bad. Dat ice cut like a razor, there be blood on the dancefloor doing that shit, that's right. But it was fun, anything where Bubbles is hanging out in dat little mothafucking bikini gotta be fun, right? Outta sight, cha'mone! Outta mothafucking sight. Same goes when we did the Suicide Dive and Bubbles had her fine little bikini on. She be a shorty, y'all wanna go skee with brother, like I said, fine pussy tang, tang, like prime cuts, cha'mone. Y'all know what I'm talking about, daaa. A check-dec-da-dec-da-cone!

SERIES TWO

So series one had gone well. So well, in fact, Channel 4 asked if I would like to do a second series. Would I?! I fucking loved it! My job for a living was now what I once did in my spare time. Celabrities are my spare time and now they were going to be other bits of time that weren't spare! On the perfect. Still quite a low key show, we decided that we would have to introduce me once more to people that still don't know who I am. So in the opening of the first episode of the second series, that's what we did. I still kept my dead mother in the wardrobe, but she was starting to stink a bit like a charity shop, maybe worse. The Craig was still in the cupboard also. He was always free to go, but he liked it there. He got to be on television every Friday night. Plus, sometimes we had a lot of fun eating crisps and drinking vodka like crazy show biz wild boys! Ozzy made a return, but his English had got better which was a concern because really his role in the show was to be more foreign than me, so I look English so all the haters out there would like me because they think that I'm actually English putting on the Arachnipusian accent. People hate Arachnipusians, especially the English. I don't know why, we don't have any refugees in your country, apart from me, we don't cause any wars over religion. Sure, we worship the slug, but I don't. In fact, I bet if you ask an English person if they have ever actually met an Arachnipusian they will say no. Unless they've met me. Bastards!

Yes, we were still filming the show in my flat, but things had got a lot more elaborate, I think. The opening of the shows were shots used in many of my favourite films. They weren't spoofs or lampoons and were probably not that obvious to the viewer, but I knew they were there. Like in the opening shot of the first episode, it was a homage to the Spider-Man movie when **Peter Parker** (or the child-faced **Tobey Maguire**), he say: "I'd like to say that is me" when a handsome man enter the screen. Then he say, "Hell I'd even take him…" and somebody else less handsome comes on the screen, then the camera lands on Peter Parker – a geeky tit-face like myself – "That's me there with the gingers". That's the kind of thing I'm talking about; it's not a spoof, just a little homage. Living out our fantasies – that's the best thing Bo' Selecta! has done for me. Basically, I live out my fantasies, it's amazing. But not more amazing than when I went to Soccer Six, which if you don't know is a celabrity football match for charity. Anyone from **Jordan** to **Michelle** from Liberty X is there, I know it's hard to believe, but it's true. Actually, I remember Jordan was there. I watched her and just waited for her to run. When she did, it was immaculate, like one of the seven wonders of the world. Well, like two of them. Her tats are bloody massive! I'd love to eat my dinner off them. Or watch television on them, or make a cake on top of them. There is so many things that you could do on them. I was so infatuated with her and them that I gave her a gift of a lady's fangitta towel, one of the ones that is like a cotton wool cigarette – a tampet I think. She wasn't impressed. But Rod Stewart was when I showed him how to _**Ram-shank**_!

The Ram-shank is a sexy dance to express your like towards someone without being too rude. It look like you're putting your fuck stick in them, but you're really just being funky, man! So it's nice, you can do it in the disco when you are on holidays in Butlins and it won't offend anyone. So Ram-shank away my very good friends! **Ram-shank**, **Ram-shank**, **Ram-shank.**

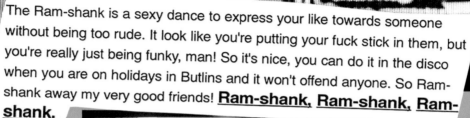

It was the second series when I developed my obsession for winner of BBC's Fame Academy, **David Sneddon**. I don't know why, it's just when I start to like someone it's all I think about. So I broke into his house. It seemed the obvious thing to do. It was easy as piss, using a coat hanger bent into the shape of Sneddon's house door key, I sneaked in like a rabbit disguised as a squirrel stealing nuts (go with it I'm spicing it up to make interesting reading, of course I didn't break in. That's illegal, it was all acting for television. His P.A. let us in). I had this strange desire to do a poo poo in his toilet. I thought it would be a great gift for him after he come home from making pop hits all day at work. Sneddon is a good man and we would later reunite for the **Christmas Single 'Proper CrimBo'**.

Meeting pop lesbians *tATu* was fun. I made them a collage of my favourite lesbians. kd lang, Anna from Big Brother 1, Pat Butcher, they were all on there. I was dressed as a lesbian myself, called Eva. I thought it would be the only way I could interest them. After presenting them with my collage they said I was the biggest lesbian they ever saw, but didn't want to lez off with me. Which was a shame. I think I could have lezzed off really well. I've watched a lot of lesbians do their stuff on the Adult Channel – nearly as good as 'Back To The Future'.

I entered a competition on the radio during the second series to meet **Brian McFadden** from Westlife. You had to write why you would like to meet him in less than 25 words. I wrote: "I would like to meet Brian from Westlife because I fucking love him, and if I don't meet him I will kill myself and then…" That's it I ran out of words, but I won the competition and I made him a Brian from Westlife Toss Bank out of masking tape so he can take it on tour with him. When his fans scream and shout at him "Aaaaaarrrrrr! I want your fucking babies Brian, you sexy bint!", they can just dip their fingers into the toss bank, get a little bit of his sex wee and stick it up them so they can have his babies. It sounds really rude and disgusting, but it's no ruder than him actually doing a sex with all his fans. His dick would drop off, they all want his babies! I know I would if I had a womb.

At Party In The Park the security treated me like a shit ball. Don't climb over the wall, don't talk to him, you can't go in there. How was I supposed to do my report if I couldn't climb over, talk to him and go in there? I think Denise Van Outen took a little shine to me. Even if she just do it out of pity for me, I don't care a shit. So I get down on one knee, saying nothing rude like a gentleman, and I ask her if she will stick her finger in my ring and marry me. She say she will think about it. I knew she wouldn't, but it was nice just to have her put her finger in my ring. It fit like a snug in a bug in a rug.

Then Rock fatty **_Meat Loaf_** came out to do the press run. It was incredible. I sing my interview to him because I was so impressed by him. "Do you have any backstage gossip?" He say, "I just wanna sell **Danni Minogue**'s underwear on e-Bay!" I say, I mean sang, "I'll give you 60 pounds right now". He sings, "5.50, or we have no deal". Then I sing back, "I would pay anything for Danni's pants, but I won't pay that!" just like he sing in his song. "I Would Do Anything For Love But I Won't Do That", and, do you know what?, I think that is the first time I have ever done a real joke. I was very happy, so I go home and do a toss. Thank you please Mr Meat, you are the best fat rock man I ever meet!

CHRIS MOYLES

I gave Chris Moyles a dog once. Everybody say, "Don't give him a dog Avid, he might be allergical." Do you know what? He was allergical! What a bastard.

Remember **ATOMIC KITTEN**? Not like I do! I got the opportunity to do a dance-off with them. The best pussy threesome I ever have. Jenny Frost slapped me in the mouth and it fucking kill me twice! But they had this great idea that when I do my dance (actually, it was a stand-in dancer who could do back flips), their nipplets would go erect. So they had these false nippies put in, which meant I could stare at them without feeling like a dirty bad boy. They were operated by air pumps that made the nipplet go on bonk. It was a beautiful thing.

Straight after that shoot I went to the 'Charlies Angels' premiere and was treated like a shit as always by security. But I said "Hello to you" to **_Drew Barrymore_**. I love her and that E.T. bastard got to kiss her. There is no way she would kiss him now that she grow up to be a fine piece of fangitta. Bastard E.T. for doing snogging with my girlfriend. I'm not mental. Drew Barrymore is funny and has great tats. Beautiful. More cute than a little kitty sat in a basket of salad.

HO! ho! HO!
ELECTA!

It was the end of the second series, but wouldn't it be great to do a Christmas Special? I love Christmas, it's even better than St George's day! So that was the next thing on the agenda. But first, how about a Christmas song? What? Me doing a Christmas song? Yes, it would be very nice, but the thing is the Cheeky Girls can sing better than me. But because it was a novelty song, it don't matter about my shit singing, as long as it is catchy and Christmassy, but not like the Tweenies or Mr Blobby. I don't like them. So I choose a song, I like 'Little Drummer Boy' by David Bowie and Bing Crosby. I write a little ditty to the tune of 'Little Drummer Boy'. The boys who do the music for the show do the music for the song, and we are shooting the video with guests; **Bob Geldof, Mel B, Holly Valance, Denise Van Outen, Terri Dwyer, Dermot O'Leary, Ade Adepitan, Caroline Flack, Kerry McFadden, Ben Shephard, Jade Goody, Chris Moyles, Edith Bowman, Jenni Falconer, Katy Hill, Chris Bisson, Kirsty Gallagher, Simon Amstell, David Sneddon, 4 Poofs And A Piano from Friday Night with Jonathan Ross, Craig Philips and Ozzy, Adam and Joe, Melanie Blatt, Harvey from So Solid, Richard Bacon, Jimmy Carr, Christine Hamilton, The 3am Girls from the newspaper, Kate Thornton, John Leslie and Mathew Wrigh**t, who didn't know they were appearing together, and we all know what happened between those two: "Who did it?", "He did it, oops…".

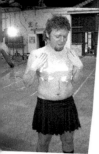

Not forgetting **DAVID GRAY** with his wobble head, who turned up for the shoot just as we heard that we don't have clearance for the song because the people that own it think that the changed lyrics are too rude. So the boys who do the music quickly come up with a different tune, but the lyrics stay the same. It was a nerving moment, but we did it in the end. The video was so exciting to do. Even though I had done two television series and appearances on shows such as T4 with the brilliant June and Vernon, Jonathan Ross (three times! He is the best, I wish I was him) and SMTV (oh Cat Deely I would cut myself for her), Top Of The Pops and Popworld with the lovely gay Simon Amstell, I still was getting (and still do get) over wellemented at what is going on with all of my life. It is easier, I think, to believe in Prince than to believe in what has happened. Because, let's face it, nobody knows that Prince is real, do they? Nobody has actually met him. He's like Jabba the Hutt from 'Return Of The Jedi'. Yes, Harrison Ford is stood there talking to him, but is he real, or is it just three children inside of him moving his mouth and eyes? Think about it, go on pause and think about it.

Amazing! Christmas 2003 Bo' Selecta's! 'Proper CrimBo' goes to number four in the charts, The Darkness at two, Kelly and Ozzy at three and that man with 'Mad World' at number one. It was a happy Christmas in the Merrion household.

Proper CrimBo

On the seven days of Christmas my true love gave to me
A Peregrine Falcon, Proper Bo I tell thee
Shell toe trainers and a beanie hat
A new set of headphones all shiny and black
I didn't sleep that night for Santa to come
I wet the bed
That's what I had done
Cos Christmas time is the place to be
I always wake up in a puddle of wee
With a ho, ho, ho!
and a silent night
A little chipolata I'll be feeling alright
Turkey's on the table as big as a cow
Celebrate CrimBo
I'll tell you how

Ho, ho, ho!
Open up your door
I got presents y'all
Bought them two by two
They closed the shop so I could buy them for you
Super soaker and dem water bombs
Watch out Santa, cos here I comes
Cos I sleep on the floor, never ever on the bed
That Santa stuff's all in your head
It's me dressed up
Come sit on my knee
I got gifts for y'all
What you got for me?
Cha'mone, cha'mone, cha'mone
Chick, chick da cone
I said Bubbles ain't a monkey
She can move real funky
Cha'mone chick, chick da cone

Come now sing with me
Proper CrimBo
I'll take you for a drink with me
Proper CrimBo
Put up your Christmas tree
Proper CrimBo
So excited you might wee
Proper CrimBo
Proper CrimBo

Come now sing with me
Proper CrimBo
I'll take you for a drink with me
Proper CrimBo
Put up your Christmas tree
Proper CrimBo
So excited you might wee
Proper CrimBo
Proper CrimBo
Proper CrimBo

AVID MERRION'S CHRISTMAS TIME

Fun, fun, fun
Fun, fun, fun
Fun, fun,
OK I write my Christmas list
A carriage clock for Jamie Oliver to time his eggs,
A flask full of my sex wee for Cat Deely,
A hedgehog-shaped doorstop for Tess Daly and Vernon Kay
I can't wait for 12 days, I wish it was today
I can't wait

I put up my tree, stick my Kylie on top
I made it myself, you can't buy it from a shop
My baubles do shine, but my lights they do not
I don't like the Minogue, but I love her a lot

So let me do tell you who else I do love
I love Edith Bowman and Liberty X
I love Misteeq with their brown shiny legs
Destiny's Child and their shiny legs

Davina McCall, but sure you know this
Her nose or fangitta I dream I do kiss
I know I am dirty, don't mean to be bad
I draw filthy pictures, I know I am sad

Christmas time is here again
Christmas time is here again

I decorate the cupboard for the Craig to enjoy
I give him a kiss and I play with his toy
I tease him with booze, and tease him with fags
I give him a present, I hire him some slags
My So Solid calendar has chocolates inside
I look for my presents, my dead mother she do hide
She buy me Westlife goodies for me
A T-shirt and a hat and I look like a twat

Christmas time is here again
Christmas time is here again
Christmas time is here again

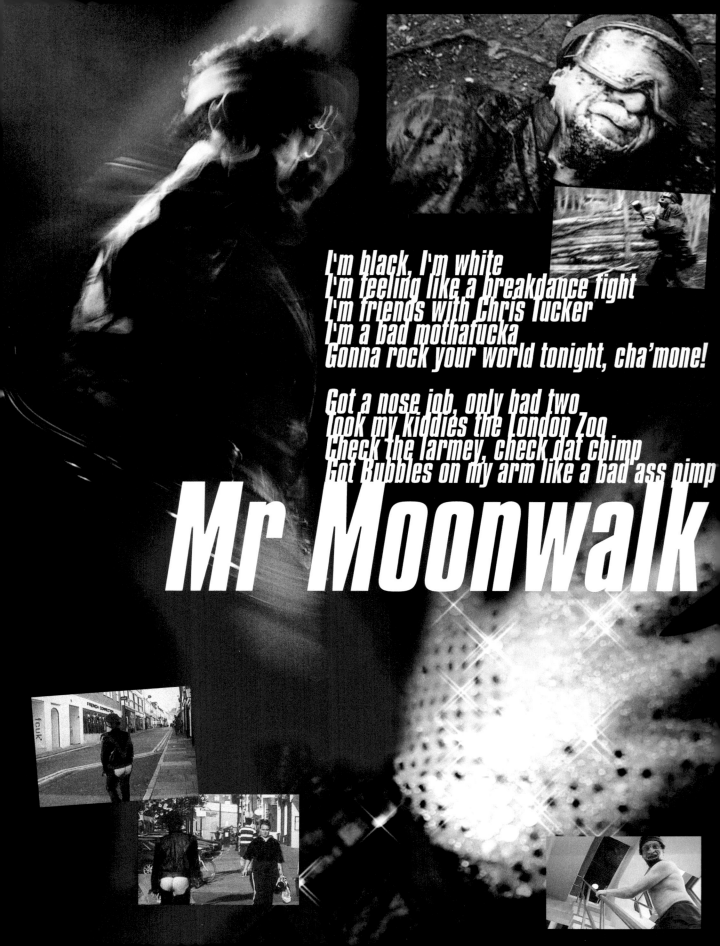

I'm black, I'm white
I'm feeling like a breakdance fight
I'm friends with Chris Tucker
I'm a bad mothafucka
Gonna rock your world tonight, cha'mone!

Got a nose job, only had two
Took my kiddies the London Zoo
Check the larmey, check dat chimp
Got Bubbles on my arm like a bad ass pimp

Mr Moonwalk

I'm a bad invincible fish food suit wearing motherfucker

Call him Mr Moonwalk
Call him Mr Moonwalk
Call him Mr Moonwalk
Call him Mr Moonwalk
Call him Mr Moonwalk
Call him Mr Moonwalk
Call him Mr Moonwalk
Call him Mr Moonwalk

Cha'mone that's right
Check this shit!

Brooke Shields, Liz Taylor
Goddamn I wanna nail her
Those big ass tits gonna do me right
Check my pants, y'all know they're tight

It won't be long 'til I'm back on top
Y'all used to call me the king of pop
Get back in the charts and it won't be long
Mothafucking press keep doing me wrong
cha'mone

The Christmas Special that went out that year was, I think, the best Bo' Selecta! to date. It felt very big. We had ***Alice Cooper, Ronan Keating, Sophie Ellis Bextor, Mel C and Sharleen Spiteri***, who unfortunately was cut out because the show was too full. That often happens, we film too much, but it's not all bad because it finishes up on the DVD. Sharleen was very nice. I met her at the MTV awards, which was also a great privilege to be asked to do. In my picture, you can see her tat tape through her dress, sexy bitch, Mmmm Scottish lovely. She said she was a fan of the show and mainly that's how we would get them on. If they were a fan, then they come on. I tried never to mock them, because that's not what I am about. I love those people like the back of my ball sack. I need that sack, you know how I speak about? I think you do. By the time we came to do the Christmas Special, **'HO, HO, HO SELECTA!'**, the show had become more television elaborate and fantasy.

Alice Cooper played the part of the ghost of Christmas yet to come as the programme was set around a spoof of 'A Christmas Carol' or 'Scrooge'. Alice showed me that in the future I'd become so obsessed with my love for celabrites that I'd forgotten the love for my dead mother, and she had gone and found herself a piece of husband pie in the form of a lady boy played by a new friend of the show, Ross Lee. He is a funny thin man that has the body of **GOLLUM** from 'The Lord of The Rings', so it was obvious that he was the man to get to play the role of Gollum in our spoof of the film, entitled 'Bored Of The Rings' as the team reassembled in early 2004 for Bo' Selecta! Vol 3.

SERIES THREE

By the time it came to doing **Bo' Selecta! Vol. 3,** it had become as normal as doing a poo poo with sweetcorn in it for me to be recognised on the tube, street or on holiday in Disney World where somebody shout at me, *'Don't say fuck or bugger!'* It was a little embarrassing, because there was a lot of children around. But I am happy that people like the show. Because I had become known in the street, though, there was no way I could go to book signings, because even the security knew me. Everyone would always ask me: how can you go on with the show now that lots of celabs know who you are? Of course, it was going to be easy because now I can get close to celabs. They all think that I am like them, I'm welcomed into their circle. But I'm not like them, I want to drink their spittle and they give me a certificate smile. Hey, it's no biggy getting your 25 metres swimming certificate, so you try to hold back your proud smile and get a wobbly mouth, this is a certificate smile.

So the format of the show had to change. I liked the idea of being a chat show host. Going on **Jonathan Ross** was great fun, but I am shit at doing the chat show host. Maybe that could be my appeal! Everybody like the underdog, and I was under the underdog. Because Ozzy had become such a friend of the show and myself, he had to come along also, but what could he do? In the past he had always made my T-shirts, so he came on board as the man in charge of wardrobe. He seemed a little different though, his clothes were cool, his wrists were limp and then the penny dropped. With his bleached hair it was staring me in the face and then looking at my buttocks, my peachy buttocks: He was a gay! But you know what? I think he make a better gay than he was a straight. He was full of fun! And he wanted to fill me and the Craig with his fun!

Craig was no longer in the cupboard. He was always free to leave. Like I say, he just wanted to be on television, and after his successful appearance on Channel 5's 'Back to Reality', where he had a hoo-har with the father of **Jade Goody**'s bambino Jeff Brazier, his popularity had upped a little, so he'd landed a TV show of his own called 'I Love Wood', accompanied by a big breasted lady called Michelle, who I'm sure Craig did a sex with. I was happy for Craig, and I was still going to see him, because they made his show in the next studio where would be filming **Bo' Selecta! Vol. 3.**

All the same team were working on Bo! Vol 3. It was nice to see everyone. **Spencer Millman** the producer who think he look like James Nesbitt, but really he look like Danny DeVito from the American sitcom 'Taxi'. He was most of the time stressed and tired and worried about how much we have to do. "We got so much to do!" is what he always say. But a happy man when he have a cigarette or six in his mouth. **BEN PALMER** the director who everybody think is gay. Hey, so what if he is? He should just come clean about it, nobody will mind unless he try to touch bums, and I'm sure his parents will still like him. I've met them, they're very nice. I myself don't think he is gay because I've seen him like ladies. Anyone who know him and is reading this, don't worry **_BEN IS NOT GAY_**. It's just a joke that we have on set. He could be though don't you think? He's handsome just like a gay.

Ben would always have us do take after take, after take; "One more while we're here." That's what he say all the time. "While we're here"? Well, we're not going to do one while we're not here, otherwise it won't be on the show. Stupid big gay. Just joking.

Debi McGrath, the assistant producer/celab booker, did a good job convincing celabs who come on the show that I wasn't going to put my wet on them. But hey, how about they put their wet on me? In Vol. 3, I think I asked almost every guest to do a spittle on me. I think if I can't put a little bit in them, then they can put a little bit in me. **SEAN PERTWEE** had really thick spit like custard. I was asking him to sign a copy of the movie he did called 'Dog Soldiers', but his pen wasn't working. So I thought "Fuck it", and said, "Why don't you just spit on me?", and he did. From then on, I asked all the guests to spit on me. On the set of Coronation Street, **Suranne Jones** spat in my face and it splashed on to *Samia Ghadie*. She asked us to please not show it, because her mother will not approve. But she wasn't worried about the fact that her mother will be watching the bit where I dry humped her in Jack and Vera's house. Isn't that strange?

You may think I am a dirty wank boy but, for the record, I have never stuck my love in a whore. I'm saving all my love for when a celebrity comes along that might find something in me that is attractive. I would only do a sex fuck with a celab. Somebody out there must like gingers – look at **Mick Hucknall** from Simply Red. I read in a magazine he has stuck it up **Martine McCutcheon**, but it made her sick up on his ginger dreadlocks. He has had some with _Catherine Zeta-Jones, Kim Wilde_ and somebody else!

MICK HUCKNALL

WALKING GINGERLY

WITH MICK HUCKNALL FROM SIMPLY RED

As a ginger man myself, growing up in the ginger ghetto,

I've experienced a lifetime of torment and name-calling. I'm no stranger to running from black, brown or blonde haired bastards that think that just because they've got a more aesthetically pleasing hair colour than myself that I'm lower than them; that I deserve to be bullied and laughed at like a funny dog that's got a bucket on its head so it can't scratch its stitches that it's had just by its eye after it's had a fight with a right fat cat that no one likes. I hate cats, what with me fair ginger skin they bring me out in red blotches.

These days, cos I'm filthy rich from my success as front man of Simply Red, I get a lot of ladies that want to put their breasts in my eyes, mouth and face, sometimes in my bloody ears, and I don't really get so much grief, but I've had my fair share. So as a thank you to all the gingers that have bought me LPs, CDs and albums, here's some handy tips to avoid violent confrontation due to your ginger appearance

Name calling will never hurt us, but sticks and stones will break our ginger bones!

THEM BASTARDS.

First off, you can always go for the simple option by wearing a nicely fashioned hat.

If you're ginger pig-sick of people calling you a Duracell, carrot-top, blood-nut, copper-top or ginger-minge, why don't you have done with it and dye your ginger hair? Now, because ginger doesn't take that well to hair dye, you may have to have it done properly at a hairdressers, rather than a DIY job at home. You'll pay through the nose, but it'll be worth it when you come out of that salon with your smart brown locks,and you can go into a pub and actually not get laughed at. And who knows, you might even get served!

Only go out at night. If it's dark enough, folk might not notice your orange tinge.

You could shave it off. But keep up with it, cos when your ginger stubble comes through, you'll be as ginger as you are bald. Then you'll be a ginger bald bastard. Do you understand what I'm saying to you with my mouth?

Wear a turban on your head.

Buy a wig if you must.

Hold an animal in front of your face. Not something too big, because you don't want to obscure your mouth; folk won't be able to understand what you're speaking about. A baby seal, a large hedgehog or badger, a peacock or an aardvark should do the trick.

Another way of using animals to disguise your gingers is to place a dead fox or squirrel on your head and add a little bit of fake blood dribbling down your forehead. You can tell people that while you were out in your garden, one of these ginger animals (because they are, they're both ginger) fell on your head. They'll feel so sorry for the squirrel or fox that they won't even notice your ginger curls wisping out from under the stinking decaying vermin. If you're talking to a lady while you're wearing either of the two on your head, tell her that you found it on the road dying, so you scraped it up with your head. If she's an animal lover she'll be so overwhelmed by your good deed she might even let you have sex with her.

If none of these methods of disguising what most people laugh at more than a fatty don't appeal to you, fuck 'em! Stand tall, be ginger and proud! Say it: I am ginger and proud! But don't come running to me if you get stoned in the street by naughty kids and they start singing "Ginger nut, ginger nut, fell in a bowl of fishes, a fish came up and gobbled him up, and that's the end of ginger nut!"

Deal with it, I know I've had to, bloody 'ell.

I WAS MICK HUCKNALL FROM SIMPLY RED.

GOOD LUCK.

Stuart the researcher on the show, whose job it was to… erm… to research, I guess, would often double up in the masks if we were doing a scene like **MICHAEL JACKSON** and <u>Ronney Barkey</u> in 'Doing Porridge'. That's Stuart doing Ronnie and doing it great, then his rubbish voice is dubbed over with my rubbish voice. Sometimes, we don't have enough time to do split screen with me playing all the parts, so Stuart do it. He also do Judy, but she don't speak. That's Judy of **'Richard & Judy'**. Judy was his best work he ever do, I think.

Auntie Trisha's

Lickle Problem Page

Hear me now, and welcome to Auntie Trisha's problem page. Dees be just some of da laters that me got where hi have hactually helped people we me advice and ting. One love!

Dear Auntie Trisha,
I'm a minority, what can I do?

Don't arks me what ta do. You should get out a bit and meet some people. Make friends with dem a lickle. Be social with other minorities. Together you won't be a minority. Unless you are terribly deformed like a monster or da helephant man. Now when I say "rice", you say, "and pee." Rice! Make you feel a lickle bit better.

Dear Trisha,
I think I have an eating disorder. For breakfast I have three sausage sandwiches and a bowl of ice-cream. For lunch I eat six burgers, large fries, an apple pie and two large milkshakes, three scotch eggs, fish and chips and a battered Mars bar.

Me tink that you do have an eating disorder. Da problem is, I fink, you be a right greedy bastard. Your batty must be so big you can't see your lickle penis. O-buntu bio, o-buntu! Go hon ha diet, yer fat bumble-squot! Buy a dog and take it for a walk a lickle bit, you lazy blood clart. Failing all of that, why don't you try Auntie Trisha's new bogle, bogle, bogle shakes or me rice and pee in da pot. You see the weight dropping off you quicker than somebody can shout, "You look like Rick Waller boi!"

Dear Auntie Trisha,
Since we've had our second child, my husband and I seem to have lost all interest in sex. What can we do?

You gotta shake your booty girl, grind it up, wind it down, do you get me? Put a bit of Shabba Ranks on in de bankground so it all romantic and ting. If Mr Lover Man don't get jiggy, get a girl in. A man can't resist two ladies munching on da carpet.
One love! Two times. Kiss me teeth. Irie!

Dear Trisha,
I'm a single woman in my late twenties and I'm worried that I have too much facial hair. Could my facial hair be the reason I'm single?

Hof course that be da reason you're single, girl! No man like to fink that he is kissing BA Baracus from da A-Team. You gotta wax it, shave it or burn it right off. You don't want to be walking round like no yeti. No man will go near yer. I fink you might have a penis and ting with testicles. Go to da saloon and git rid. Now I say "Rice", you say "and pee". Come along, come along sing with me. When I say "Rice", you say "and pee!" Rice…

trisha's
Bogle, Bogle, Bogle Shake
Peppered Shrimp
FLAVOUR

meal

The other researchers were the lovely Kate and James. Hard-working James did such a great job when we were shooting in America. He was so tired after we finish at 3am in the morning on the last night that he left his cash card in the machine. He was so fucked off, but cheered up a little when we went back to the pub opposite the hotel that we were staying at and had birthday drinks for myself. I couldn't believe it. The American people are so nice. I'd only been in the pub once, but Ben and James told them that at the end of the week it was my birthday. Who would have thought it? Me, Avid Merrion, celabrating my birthday in the U.S of America with a bunch of strangers! They're great people, apart from **_ROSS_** **from 'Friends'**. While we were taking a break, we spotted Ross from 'Friends'. I got so excited I think a bit of wet come out. So I go up to him and ask him if I could thank you please have a photo with him. **_But he say, "NO, I don't do photos!" He fucking does_**! I see him on the cover of the DVD of 'Friends'. I saw him again later in the year at the Glamour awards where I was presenting an award to the lovely 'Girls Aloud'. But I didn't ask him for a photo this time, **_bitch_**..

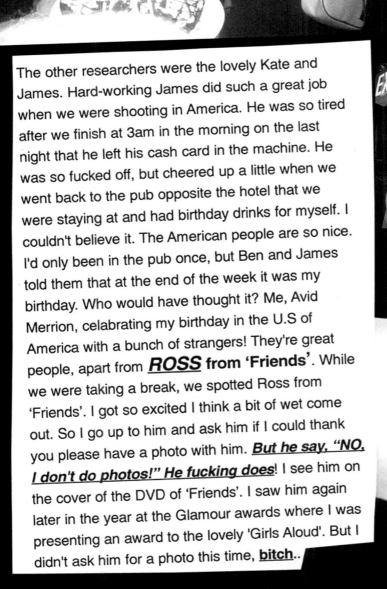

AVID ON BOOZE

My first memory of drinking alcohol: I was in cupboard drinking cider, I think I was about 12 years of age and I can't remember if I was with a blow-up doll or a real girl, but it was very reminiscent of that scene in **'Teen Wolf'** (Shit! All I do is talk about that fucking film!), you know, when he is in a wardrobe with a dark haired girl – Booth I think her name was. Anyway, he get so carried away trying to stick his love inside her that he rip all her dress. That's what I did, I ripped all the girl's dress and then she went all soft. That's why I think maybe it was a blow-up girl, I burst her. Crazy days. We were so drunk, like out of space. But hey, we were kids, right? Stupid kids.

Now I mostly drink lager, vodka, water, Iron-bru, Tizer, soup, white wine that don't cost more than six English pounds and celabrity spittle. Spirits? I like Slimer from **'GHOSTBUSTERS'**! Ha! Ha! Ha! Ha! And Michael Hutchence! Ha! Ha! Ha! I like vodka, thank you please.

Screw tops are being increasingly used by some top wine producers, I like screw tops because you can screw them. So many times I have tried to be cool like ***Crocodile Dun-dee*** and tried to crack open a beer on a desk corner, but just smashed the bottle and looked like a prat. You don't want to get so drunk you don't know what you are doing, because you might try be cool like Dun-dee and end up cutting your lips open drinking out of a smashed bottle and then you will look really shit, I think.

Patsy Kensit's love life has been well-documented, but she's always tried to keep her friendship with ex-Spice Girl Mel B under cover. Here she shares the covers with the scary one, who has recently been said to be more than just good friends with the Lethal Weapon 2 star. But what really goes on under Kensit's posh Egyptian cotton sheets?

WHEN PATSY MET MEL
'THE ODD COUPLE' OPEN THEIR HEARTS TO BO' SELECTA!

Not since Jordan and Peter Andre were named the new Posh and Becks has such an 'odd couple' as Patsy Kensit and Mel B been so likely to capture the nation's heart as the next big celebrity couple. It wasn't until the Christmas special of Bo' Selecta!, cleverly titled 'Ho, Ho, Ho Selecta!', that they came face-to-face for the first time. Mel B had often chatted to the Bo' Selecta! crew about her fondness for blonde Patsy, but no one could have imagined that the chemistry between the two ladies that was so apparent on set would lead to the two female stars moving in together. Close friends deny that there's anything more to their relationship than "just good friends". Some would say that they are more than just good friends – an inside source said that the two have a special relationship, similar to E.T. and Elliot in which the cute alien could feel the young boy's emotions, whereas with Mel and Patsy Mel feels Patsy's breasts like a massive lesbian. Some claim that the alleged lesbian affair is just a PR stunt to promote the new series of Bo' Selecta! which airs Friday June 18th, 10.30pm on C4. So are Mel and Patsy to become the new tATu ?

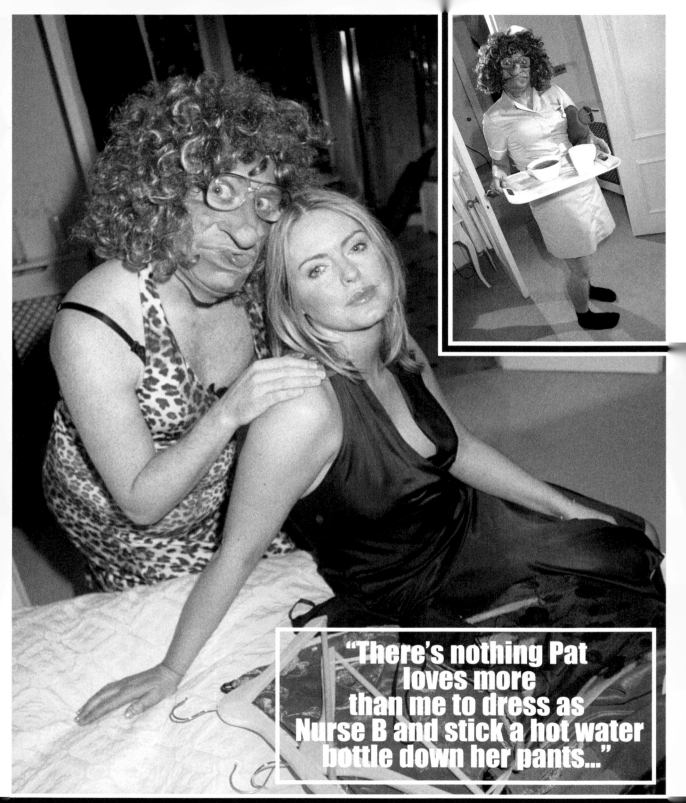

"There's nothing Pat loves more than me to dress as Nurse B and stick a hot water bottle down her pants..."

Above Mel wears trademark leopard print dress, while Patsy gets ready to go out, but will Mel B be coming out with her, or will she be kept in the closet with the rest of Patsy's fancy frocks? True love or lesbian lust? **Inset** Mel spices up Pat's life waiting on her hand-and-foot in her kinky nurse guise **Opposite (top)** Bath time: Mel patiently waits for Patsy's towel to fall off **Opposite**

At home with Beauty and the Beast

So Mel, it's been reported in the press that you prefer the company of a woman. Is this the result of a string of rocky relationships, and are you done with men?

Mel: The thing is love, Pat has helped me out more than any man has in the past. Firstly, she let me move in with her at a time when things were hard for me. Cos I've been trying to get Spices back together, but Vicki in't having any of it. Well, she don't need to work does she? She's got Dave to live off of. As for me, I haven't got Sky Digital in every room like I used to. I've got a black and white portable and I have to make do. But she's very good to me is our Pat. From letting me share her posh Dolcy Gabardos frocks to putting cream on me grapes for me, she's always there for me. As a woman, a gorgeous one at that, she understands a woman's needs.

We have a great time together, sometimes we'll just spend a quiet night in and watch a video. Just the other night we watched that 'Showgirls', fook me it was fantastic! What was it Pat?

Pat: It was rubbish.

Mel: She loved it, it were a right breast fest. I had to go to the bog to sort meself out half-way through. I've got an high sex drive, yer see. Even watching Emmerdale, I have to watch it out of the road of the kids, in a room by meself. I just get carried away, especially now that our Pat's in it. Here, she nearly caught me t'other day, though, din't yer love?

Patsy: You're disgusting.

Mel: Yeh, I had me little cucumber friend out and everything, in a world of me own I was, curtains were shut and I was having the time of me life. Oh I love our Pat in Emmerdale, she's a right cow!

We had some great guests in the Vol. 3. In the first episode, we had the lovely **<u>Emma Bunton</u>**. She was really into it. I went up to her dressing room to meet her and get all my bad swearing and filth out of the way so I wouldn't say too much dirty when she was on set. I wanted to desensitise her to it all, and it worked. Once on the set, she was willing to play *Spot My Balls*. It's just like Spot The Ball where you have to draw a cross where you think the ball is. She had to make a cross where she thought my balls were on the pictures that we had enlarged from the little sexy booklet that come with her album. She giggles and would play it coy, but I said to her when the cameras weren't filming, "Everybody think you are sweet like a little baby, but I bet you are a dirty bad slut girl, right? You sexy bitch." I can't tell you what she said, but she left the studio happy, and I'm sure she doesn't hate me. The next time I see her, I will say "hello to you" to her.

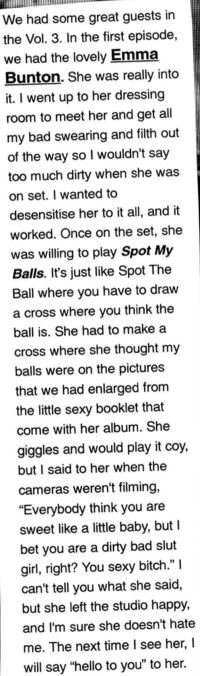

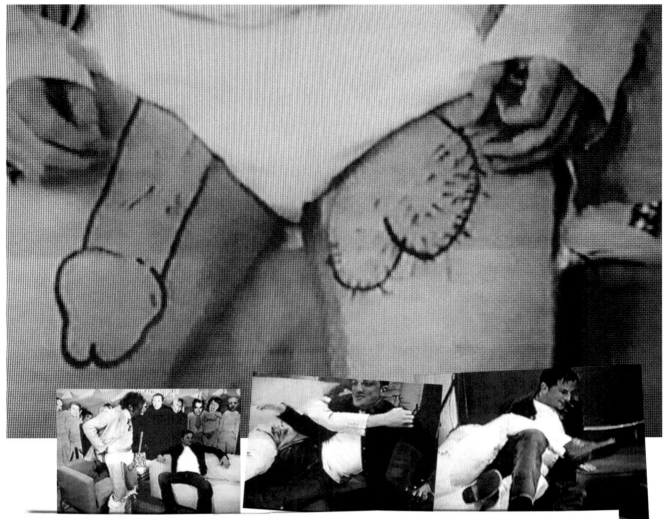

Peter Andre was next. This was good because he had never seen the show, so it could go all kinds of ways. I think he was still excited about his new success. He jumped all over the set like a little boy who has had too many E numbers in his food. Don't give him chocolate! He will go crazy like a mad bastard. I was amazed when he said the word c*nt. He said that in the jungle, when he met Jordan in 'I'm A Celabrity, Get Me Out Of Here', that he was c*nt drunk. But he assured me it wasn't her massive tats that he fell for, it was her personality. That's the reason I love Jordan, it's nothing to do with her big beautiful tats. It's the sweet-mannered alter ego Katie Price that I adore. Katie who like to ride little ponies. Not ***dirty sex monster*** **Jordan** who would rather suck a stallion's big veiny cock. Who am I kidding? I like both Jordan and Katie and **JACK OSBOURNE**. Jack was the next guest. He was a great fun. We filmed the piece on top of the hotel that we were staying at. The manager said he couldn't close it to the public, but they soon left when I told Jack what I would do if **Kylie Minogue** was my wife.

"If ***Kylie*** was my wife, I would treat her with the respect that a wife deserve. I would have her at my beck and call, she would bring my slippers, make my food, and at the end of the day I would ask her to take her clothes off, but keep on her belt so I could ride her like Seabiscuit."

Then with my visual demonstration of my riding technique, the roof of the hotel was cleared of the public in seconds.

The lovely **JUNE SARPONG** came on the show with her shiny lips, and of course I demonstrated my love for Sean Pertwee with a blow-up doll. These are all people that I have had obsessions for, and now they were sat opposite me and I could ask them anything I want. I went to Coronation Street and was shown around the set by the beautiful **Suranne Jones** and **Samia Ghadie** who I mentioned earlier. But then I couldn't believe it (how many times have I said I couldn't believe it?), anyhow, I couldn't believe it when Ozzy and Sharon invited us to their mansion in Buckinghamshire.

Meet the **fu**
Parents

Ɪ10:15:43:12

Ɪ10:15:59:19

Ɪ10:16:59:17

I had drawn pictures and had them made into slides of two different dates I would like to take **KELLY OSBOURNE** on, but first I had to get the permission from her parents; Sharon and Ozzy. On the way to their fuck-off big old mansion, I began to get nervous and had a similar sweat on my brow to what **Michael J Fox** had when he was changing into one of the Planet Of The Apes and about to discover that his father is a Care Bear in the movie – yes, 'Teen Wolf'. I felt sick, so I had a shit. After I'd returned from my business trip and made a large deposit, I felt a lot better.

I'd already met them before, but it is still quite nerve-wracking meeting the **_Prince of Darkness_**. Jack was around, so that made it easier. Jack promised he would get me a Teen Wolf T-shirt, and he did. Did I mention that is one of my best films? This is how nice these people were. I could've loved him up the bum for that T-shirt. Ozzy wandered around just like he do in the **OSBOURNE** TV show, while we wait for Sharon to have her make-up done. Most of the time I would go through several times what I was going to do with Ben the director. It was all in place; I had my gift of swiss roll and beans in a plastic container for each of them. I just hoped I didn't go ruin it all with my dirty gob by saying something like, "I want to do a sex wee on your daughter's face". Sharon came down the stairs and I tell you this, she is one sexy fox. You don't expect it when you see her on television, but wowyeepyayayous! She has these eyes that look right into you and stick up your ass where your love button is.

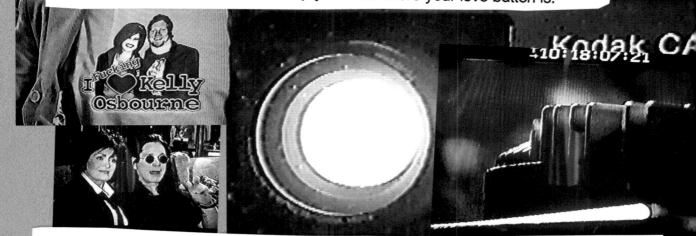

I LOVE SHARON. So it turned out they were both just as dirty (or more) as me with their mouths. Sharon spoke about the first time she meet Ozzy with his hard dick that was like a snooker cue. We had a good laugh! They didn't care too much for the Swiss roll and beans, but they gladly spat in my face. And if you watch, you can see Ozzy's spittle come straight up from the heart! It was brown. I still haven't had a date with Kelly, but Sharon gave me her number! Not Kelly's, Sharon's. Just the other week she left a message on my phone saying she would like a bit of time alone with me to suck me off at the hinge end. No really! She did. I don't think she meant it, she has a great sense of humour. I think she was having a joke and fuelling my fantasies at the same time. So now I don't know who makes me get a feeling most; Kelly or Sharon. Anyway, the two dates I'd planned for Kelly went like this:

I take Kelly to the cinema to see a romantic comedy starring Ben Stiller. While continuing to laugh and cry at **_Ben Stiller_**, I pop popcorn into Kelly's mouth. I have my penis in the popcorn box as an invitation to get closer. I don't know her that well, so I think it's better this way. I don't want to thrust it into her hand. she might think it's too forward.

I walk her home, I give her a rose. Kiss her on the cheek, then I go.

Date 2 is a little more exciting, so she probably like it more. It's the kind of date **Johnny Depp** or somebody from Limp Bizkit would take her on.

OK, I take her for a meal at Burger King. While she is munching on meat, a bog-eyed tramp is hassling her for her autograph. So I say to him, "Hey! Don't speak to my bitch when she is munching on meat. Do you want to get your head killed in?" So I grab his nostrelites and I shoot him 'til he is so dead he don't move. ***BANG, BANG!*** Then he quiver a little so I stand on his head like Bruce Lee do in 'Enter the Dragon'.

"Oooooooowoooooh!" But a bit of blood has sprayed on to Kelly's meat, so I buy her another burger, but this is how I impress her: I go Large! Kelly is so impressed I think I see a little bit of nipplet pop out.

So after we bury the body like a scenario out of the movie 'Heathers' starring CHRISTIAN SLATER and sexy tea leaf *__Winona Ryder__*, I walk her home. We take our clothes off, I give her a rose, kiss her on the cheek and fuck right off. But while I am fucking right off, I'm treating her mean and keeping her keen. I'm so mean I punch a child in the face and take his money. But I'm not a bad man. I've hired this little guy, we're in cahoots! And while I walk off, I dance. Because the ladies like a man who can dance and kill a man for their love.

Thank you please.

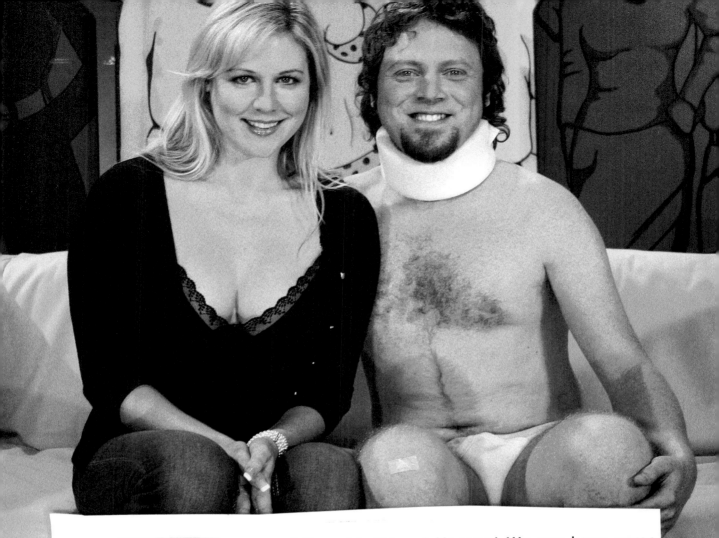

When Abi Titmuss came on I thought, "Hooo! Haaaaa! We can have some fun here." This sexy celab like to talk about sex and filth more than me. She make me look like a little choir boy. In the show we always know there is a line, this time we went passed it. She wasn't happy, a lot was cut out of the studio interview and I promised I don't speak about it. But all I can say is ~~would the type of funny thing and she~~ ~~an object and a person~~ ~~I will say. This isn't a kiss~~ ~~the legal department~~ ~~always stopped us from~~ ~~thing~~ k at some nice photo

TeenWolf

For the last episode of Vol. 3, we opened with – you've guessed it – a **'TEEN WOLF'** spoof! I played the role of MICHAEL J FOX as Scott Howard in the **Beavers** basketball team playing against the Minges. I like the word minge for the fangitta, it sound nice and cuddly. I'd like to cuddly a minge, Kylie's minge would be my favourite. We were all wearing nappies, just as we did in the Crappy Days sketch. As I was tackled to the ground by minges, I was to change into one of the most uncomfortable costumes I ever worn. I burst out from the huddle of beavers and minges as Teen Wolf. It was very hot and itchy and not the kind of costume you want to being wearing on a hot summer's afternoon, eating your lunch (a big hot chicken korma). My ass felt like it had a tap up it and my balls felt like they were in a cup of English tea. The Bear was taking over this episode, I think, due to the fact that he was better than me and more people liked him. I enjoyed the bit he did with Charlie from Busted.

hELLO RASI-CLARTS

Yes, I was very good with Charlie from Busted, wasn't I? But you must understand that in that sketch when I started crying at the end wanting my guitar back, I wasn't really crying, I was acting, and bloody good at it I was, as well. I was also good when I was doing my Gordon Ramsay impression at Jamie Oliver. Jesus, I didn't half give him some stick. I didn't mean it, though. What was I like? Fuck this, fuck that, oh I was untold.

Me and Bob Mortimer, that was a good one as well. Nice man that Bob Mortimer. It was strange sat there in the pub with him, sharing the view of Lindsey Dawn McKenzie's whopping boobies as she played the part of the bra maid, I mean bar maid.

I was also very good with Fern and Philip on this morning. Apparently, he sometimes calls her fuck face, we had that in the script originally – Philip calling Fern a fuck face. But they so rightly said, "Let's not say that", and how right they were. It was the only piece I've done that didn't have bad language in it, and to be honest with you, I thought it was brilliant. OK, I said funt and bunt and twarty-virgitus, but they're not swear words, are they? What else? Oh yeah! I showed Lisa Stansfield my tail, fun-spunked in Paul McKenna's face, and had sex with Mylene Klass, It was Shat-Pank – that means good. It's crazy talk from the street.

CRAIG DAVID

Reeto, Craig David here still in a Book' Selecta! So, as we all know I've tried me hardest at breaking America, but it just didn't happen. I don't think they're ready for Craaaaaig Daaaavid yet. Me rhymes are so sick that not even the dopiest of producers such as David Morales can chisel me nisel with me phat beats. But the shorties dig it the most. Gonna goo skeet skeet and get me some good brain. That's all American jargon for I'm so proper Bo that all't lasses fancy me, I tell thee.
Can I get a rewind?
So here are the words to me song 'Soda Pop' that I tried breaking America with. To be honest with yer, this will probably be the next song I release in't UK.
So learn all't words so you can sing along when it gets to number 1.

Bo' Selecta!

Soda Pop

by Craig David.

Sick of hangin' with hoochy mamas that think
   they are all that
With their pretty faces and their big arses behinds,
   but up front they are all flat chested
I lick like a girl all full and plump, don't care
   if her boobs are fake
She better taste fine, when I go to dine
   down on her lady cake
Cake. Piece of cake, on a plate   yum yum!
   Thats a metaphor
   for your puni
I want your honey
  On me face
You taste quite nice but you're a disgrace

Soda pop...
Come on, lets get busy
Soda pop...
Drink some of my fizzy
Soda pop...
come on lets get busy girl
Soda pop...
Drink some of my fizzy
Pop.

I don't care for tits
you boobless bitch
  Your body'll do just fine
I like your face
Your chin is ace!

... cont'd →

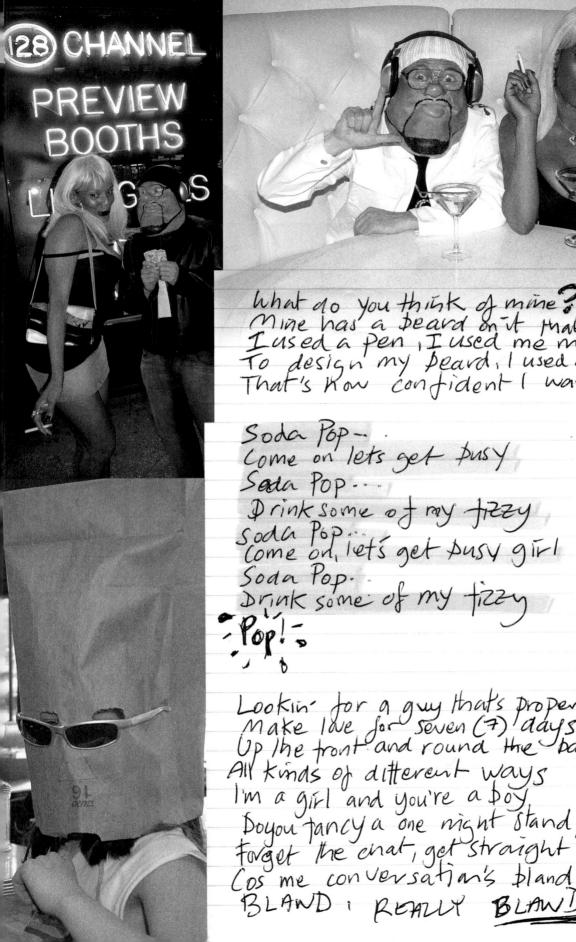

What do you think of mine?
Mine has a beard on it that I designed
I used a pen, I used me mind
To design my beard, I used a pen
That's how confident I was

Soda Pop—.
Come on lets get busy
Soda Pop—.
Drink some of my fizzy
Soda Pop...
Come on, let's get busy girl
Soda Pop.
Drink some of my fizzy
Pop!

Lookin' for a guy that's proper bo!
Make love for seven (7) days
Up the front and round the back
All kinds of different ways
I'm a girl and you're a boy
Do you fancy a one night stand?
Forget the chat, get straight to SEX
Cos me conversation's bland
BLAND, REALLY BLAND

..Cont'd

128 CHANNEL
PREVIEW
BOOTHS

CRAIG DAVID
Soda pop

Soda Pop.
Come on, let's get busy
Soda Pop
Drink some of my fizzy
Soda Pop
Come on, let's get busy girl
Soda Pop
Drink some of my fizzy
: POP :

Big busters
small busters
No busters
Ghostbusters!
i aren't afraid of no cake
Who you gonna call?
'CRAIG DAVID'

Soda Pop
Come on, let's get busy
Soda Pop
Drink some of my fizzy
Soda Pop
Come on, lets get busy girl
Soda Pop
Drink some of my fizzy
: POP :

craig C david

THE CREW

Pete Rowe
James de Frond
Annie King

Stuart Unwin
Jo Walters
Debi McGrath
Hannah Linnen

Phil Oats
Hannah Woffenden
Suzanne Knight
Charlie Fawcett

Spencer Millman
Ben Palmer
Avid Merrion
Ryan Mootoo

We had a wrap party for the final show that was supposed to be a fancy dress party according to Ozzy who, when I arrived, was wearing a dress that was fancy. Not a fancy dress costume! **_DENISE VAN OUTEN_** was to be my date. I love her in the ass and mouth. **The Liberty X** girls Jessica, Kelly and Michelle turned up, and **JODIE MARSH** in her legendary belts outfit. It was the deluxe sparkle version instead of the camo belts. She looked like a wet dream, it was very hard to look into her eyes when her nipplets were giving me so much attention winking at me. Apparently, she gave Debi the assistant producer her telephone number to give to me. I don't know what happened to it. The next time I see Jodie Marsh half-naked at a premiere, I'm going to wrestle her to the ground and let her have her way with me. I will kiss her right from her funny nose down too her lady's tongue between her legs. Oh, hold on for one moment: I have to do a thing…

Sorry about that, but when I start thinking about Jodie Marsh I have to do two things; empty my love and then draw a picture so I don't do something illegal. But don't worry, I'm not a dirty bad boy. *I love you Jodie Marsh* in the face, twice!

The last show felt like a good ending to a great series, even if some of the website people thought it was shit. I never understood fan sites where they slag everything off. Why are they fans of shit they don't like? When I am a fan of something, every toss I do I have that show, movie, pop star, actor, actress, celab in mind. I eat them, I drink them, I shit them out and draw pictures of them. **I fucking *love* celabrities**, I am an obsessive fan of celabrities, I am a celabrity stalker and I always will be. Who am I? I'm Avid Merrion. If you see me in the street say hello to you to me. I'm not a stranger, I'm no danger. I'm your friend. Thank you please. I love you in the face twice. Goodbye.

Author	Message

☐ Posted: Fri Jun 25, 2004 11:20 pm   Post subject: volume 3 is awful   Quote

god this series sucks compared to the last two the only thing that made me laugh was the richard and judy thing on tonight's. the tinned laughter is annoying and it seem's like he's desperately trying to make us laugh but it is'nt working. the chat show thing is shit as it's always him going I've got a hard one or something it's getting old already and it's only on the second week! what happened to the bear? he used to be funny but he's not anymore, grr give us the old bo selecta! 😾 I think they must be running out of idea's!!

Back to top   Profile   PM   Home   AIM   Yahoo   MSN

☐ Posted: Sat Jun 26, 2004 6:46 am   Post subject: Quote

I entirely agree, the porridge bit is the only funny bit, there are possibly a few others.

Back to top   Profile   PM   E-mail   Home   AIM   Yahoo   MSN   ICQ

☐ Posted: Sat Jun 26, 2004 12:14 pm   Post subject: Quote

🙁
Totally agree with me Julie, it sucks bigtime! The new format is crap - way too random and haphazzard. And as for the content, well it seems like it was just thrown together in five minutes for the sake of running a third series. What's with all the nob jobs and profanity? Come on guys you're funnier than that!

😾 Or are we just going to get Chubby Brown on a Friday night (God Forbid!!)

Back to top   Profile   PM

☐ Posted: Mon Jun 28, 2004 5:12 pm   Post subject: Quote

The humour's getting cruder...probably becuase its easier to write. To me that spit thing was really scraping the barrel. And Peter Andre looked as if he fell off that sofa on purpose.

———

You see, beneath my dark satanic exterior, I'm actually as soft as...POO POO

☐ Posted: Sat Jun 26, 2004 9:39 pm   Post subject: Quote

wrote:

🙁
Totally agree with me Julie, it sucks bigtime! The new format is crap - way too random and haphazzard. And as for the content, well it seems like it was just thrown together in five minutes for the sake of running a third series. What's with all the nob jobs and profanity? Come on guys you're funnier than that!

😾 Or are we just going to get Chubby Brown on a Friday night (God Forbid!!)

yeh the whole thing just seem's rushed, I think they should have properly thought this out before putting it back on air they need a better script, I don't think I shall be watching bo selecta again as it's a waste of my life!

Back to top   Profile   PM   Home   AIM   Yahoo   MSN

☐ Posted: Sat Jun 26, 2004 10:04 pm   Post subject: Quote

I think the new series OK, parts of it still makes me laugh.

tutacanaras
BO' Junior!

Posted: Fri Sep 03, 2004 11:58 am   Post subject:

its just disgusting, since when was a bear's erection funny?

Joined: 25 Jun 2004

SystemOfADownFan
BO' Newbie!

Posted: Fri Sep 03, 2004 5:21 am   Post subject:

The Bear, its the same thing every week, rude joke, penis pops out, call his squirell a ginger c**t. I just sit there stone faced waiting for the next scene (come save me Walking Gingerly).

Joined: 22 Aug 2004
Posts: 33
Location: London, UK

"I've always been a fan of Carol Smillie...it were her that got me inta DIY...I put that shelf up meself! I don't need no bloke...I love doing it meself....ooooh crab paste!" - Mel B

Back to top   Profile   PM

Posts: 85
Location: Northampton

Back to top

Profile   PM   E-mail   Home   AIM   Yahoo   MSN   ICQ

Richay
BO' Junior!

Posted: Fri Sep 03, 2004 4:49 pm   Post subject:

Ah come on dont be so harsh on the Bear, yeah he was very weak in series 3 but he was Gold in series 1 and 2 plus the short commentary on the series 1 dvd with the bear is hysterical.

Joined: 26 May 2004
Posts: 157

Site- www.geocities.com/richiespalace2003

---

spam javelin
BO' Newbie!

Posted: Mon Jul 12, 2004 9:08 pm   Post subject:

y'all is living in da past ,muvverfukkers!
ya'all dont like new charactay!!!
go watch da old DVDay chamone!
Dis is da new shit...so go suck on a cola cubay!!!
CHECK DAT SHIT!! 😈
😃😃😃😃😃😃😃😃😃😃

Joined: 10 Jun 2004
Posts: 34
Location: East London :-)~

Back to top

Profile   PM

---

higuys
BO' Newbie!

Posted: Mon Jul 12, 2004 9:44 pm   Post subject:

you are pathetic.

Joined: 11 Jun 2004

To Everybody, thank you please

Jill Francis
My Family
Ade Adepitan
Alan Buckley
Alex Fearns
Alex Hutchinson
Alice Cooper
All my friends' birds
Andrew Newman
Andrew Smedley
Andy Carroll
Annie King
Ash Atalla
Atomic Kitten
Abi Titmus
Barbara Windsor
Beatrice Gay
Ben Hall
Ben Palmer
Ben Shepherd
Bob Mortimer
Brian Cox
Camilla Smith
Caroline Flack
Catalina Guirado
Charlie Fawcett
Charlie Simpson
Chris Moyles
Christian Walsh
Christine Hamilton
Claudine Taylor
Craig David
Craig Phillips
Damon Beesley
Dan Mazer
Dave Carter
David Gray
David Morales
David Sneddon
David Tuck
David Whyte
Davina McCall
Debi McGrath
Denise Van Outen
Derek Acora
Dermot O'Leary
Doug Goddard
Ed Arriens
Edith Bowman
Emma Bunton
Ethan Hawke
Everyone at John Noel
Management, especially

Fu Olaseinde
Geraint Owen
Girls Aloud
Hannah Linnen
Hannah Woffenden
Har Mar Superstar
Hayley Finch
Ian Pearce
Ian Whitaker
Jack Osbourne
Jade Goody
James Bobin
James De Frond
Jamie Oliver
Jennifer Ellison
Jenni Falconer
Jenny Hay
Jeremy Edwards
Jimmy Carr
Jodie Marsh
Joe Walters
John Cole
John Turner
Jonathan Ross
Karen Hayley
Kate Daughton
Kate Thornton
Kathy Dyton
Keith Branch
Keith Duffy
Keith Lemon (for letting me steal his identity)
Kelly Osbourne
Kerry McFadden
Kevin French
Larry Deacon
Liberty X
Lipsync Post
Lisa Stansfield
Marise Sate
Mark Hiney
Marriella Frostrup
Matthew Ferris
Meatloaf
Mel B
Mel C
Melanie Blatt
Michael Ball
Michael Drury
Mis-teeq
Mylene Klass
Nadine
Neil Barnes

Patsy Kensit
Paul Alexander
Paul Angunawela
Paul Garner
Paul McKenna (Sorry about the shirt)
Paul Young
Penny Smith
Pete Rowe
Peter Andre
Peter Fincham
Phil Clarke
Phil Oates
Rachel Jenkins
Richard Drew
Richard Pell
Robert Popper
Ronan Keating
Ross Lee
Roy Estabrook
Russell Brand
Ryan Mootoo
Sally Debonnaire
Sally Grey
Samia Ghadie
Sarah Cawood
Sean Pertwee
Sharleen Spiteri
Sharon Osbourne
Shaun Naylor
Simon Hornbrook
Siobhan Harper Ryan
Sophie Ellis-Bextor
Spencer Austin
Spencer Millman
Steve Rees
Steve Webster
Steven K Amos
Stuart Unwin
Suranne Jones
Suzanne Knight
Tayyaba Irtizaali
Terri Dwyer
Tess Daly
Tom Stewart
Tom Thurston-Matthews
Val Ackrill
Venessa Feltz
Vernon Kay
Vicky Winter
Westlife
Will Cross

Dedicated to
Thomas Spencer Francis

Are you looking at my bird?

All photographs appear courtesy of the author except the following: Burn-Forti Dan/Corbis Sygma p.66 (left); Firooz Zahedi/JBG/Idols Licensing and Publicity Ltd p.69; Karl Grant/Idols Licensing and Publicity Ltd p.14; Kent News & Picture/Corbis Sygma p.39 (James Redmond and Nick Pickard); Ray Burmistow/Idols Licensing and Publicity Ltd p.22; Rex Features p.13 (bottom left, bottom right), 15, 17, 23, 36, 38 (Duncan James), 39 (John Leslie, Kevin Sacre); Rufus F. Folkks/Corbis p.93 (David Schwimmer); Rune Hellestad/ Corbis p.37 (Matt Goss), 38 (Peter Andre), 68 (top); Seth Joel/Corbis p.38 (Justin Timberlake); Adam Lawrence p.53 (Davina McCall)

BO' SELECTA! VOL 3
THE COMPLETE THIRD SERIES
DOUBLE DISK WITH OVER 3 HOURS OF EXTRAS